Praise for *Mom Enough*

"I can confidently say there are no words that make me breathe easier than the words of Rachel Marie Martin. No matter how long you've guilt-tripped yourself, neglected your needs, or abandoned your dreams, this compassionate guide offers real hope. Through relatable struggles and heartfelt honesty, Rachel shows us how to honor ourselves throughout our motherhood journey. Let *Mom Enough* bring peace to your soul and more of YOU to the brave story of your life."

—*Rachel Macy Stafford, New York Times* bestselling author, speaker, and special education teacher

"Rachel Marie Martin is a genius observer and storyteller of the human condition. Her writing reaches deep into the heart while allowing us to feel seen, heard, and soothed. *Mom Enough* is highly recommended and one you will come back to over and over again."

—Shonda Moralis, MSW, LCSW, Coach, Psychotherapist, and Author of *Breathe, Mama, Breathe: 5-Minute Mindfulness for Busy Moms* and *Don't Forget to Breathe: 5-Minute Mindfulness for Busy Women.*

"Rachel's *Mom Enough* is the warm hug we all need to get us through those tough days of motherhood. Whether you are in the exhausting first moments of the newborn stage or the emotional roller coaster of the teen years, this collection of heartfelt letters will make you feel less alone in your journey. In a world that is always telling us to do more and be more, Rachel reminds us that we are *already* enough—and that is a gift we should all keep giving ourselves."

—Whitney Fleming, co-owner, *Parenting Teens & Tweens*, Author and Creator behind *Whitney Fleming Writes*

"Rachel's words resonate—with the new mom, the tired mom, the single mom, the empty-nester and more. These letters articulate what so many women feel through the various seasons of motherhood. You will feel her heart as you read these letters and be reminded you aren't alone."

—*Jenn Hamrick*, Founder of *Story Social Media*

"Rachel Marie Martin has spent many years telling the truth about motherhood, including all the beautiful and not-so-beautiful moments and messes. She has put voice to the inner dialogue of millions and encouraged them to embrace their truest self. With *Mom Enough*, she has assembled a collection of the most insightful and inspiring of her poignant and authentic messages.

—Joyce Shulman, author of *Walk Your Way to Better,* and Co-Founder and CEO of 99 Walks and Jetti Fitness

RACHEL MARIE MARTIN

Founder of Finding Joy

MOM
ENOUGH

Inspiring Letters for the Wonderfully Exhausting but Totally Normal Days of Motherhood

Dexterity, LLC
604 Magnolia Lane
Nashville, TN 37211

Printed in the United States of America.

First edition: 2023
10 9 8 7 6 5 4 3 2 1

ISBN: 978-1-947297-82-1 (Hardcover)
ISBN: 978-1-947297-83-8 (E-book)

Publisher's Cataloging-in-Publication Data
Names: Martin, Rachel Marie, author.
Title: Mom enough : inspiring letters for the wonderfully exhausting but totally normal days of motherhood / by Rachel Marie Martin.
Description: Nashville, TN: Dexterity, 2023.
Identifiers: ISBN: 978-1-947297-82-1 (hardcover) | 978-1-947297-83-8 (ebook) | 978-1-947297-84-5 (audio)
Subjects: LCSH Motherhood--Anecdotes. | Parenting. | Child rearing--United States--Anecdotes. | Families--United States--Anecdotes. | BISAC FAMILY &RELATIONSHIPS / Parenting / Motherhood
Classification: LCC HQ769 .M37 2023 | DDC 649/.1--dc23

Interior Photos taken by Hannah Nicole Martin
Some Interior images used under license from Pexels

Cover design by twoline STUDIO

To my husband, Dan, who has believed in my dreams even before I could articulate them. I love you and am grateful to walk this life journey with you.

contents

introduction

It's been almost twenty-seven years since I became a mom.

I've written that, deleted that, written it again, deleted it again, stared at it, mulled it over, deleted it, and finally concluded that those words are the perfect sentence to start this book. Twenty-seven years, friends. Almost three decades. How can it be that long? How can it be that short? How can I be the one sharing such an incredible length of time when it feels like almost yesterday that I became a mom? How can I feel so young and old at the same time? Along my motherhood journey I began writing letters and posting them on my blog or on social media hoping to encourage other moms in their own journey. I still can't believe its been so many years ago.

Yet all those years ago, my identity instantly transformed from Rachel to include Mom.

Mom. Their person. Their constant. Their rock. *Their* mom.

I'm the one on the emergency contact list, the one they look for in the auditorium, the one they slam doors on, and the one they think is too strict one moment and the greatest the next. I'm the one they need when thunder shakes the house or when they lose a friend, the one who finds dinners, shoes, and missing homework pages. And I'm the one who writes the Tooth Fairy notes, lunchbox notes, and teacher notes. The one who laughs at bad jokes and shares favorite movies. I am the one who plans vacations. I am also the one who sits in auditoriums waiting for a glimpse of their face in a crowd. I am there for them in ways they might not ever even see, acknowledge, or appreciate.

I'm not perfect; I don't have it together all the time, nor do I have all the answers, and yes I even makes mistakes. I am just a mom. A human, showing up, giving of herself for those younger humans I've raised for over half of my life.

Before I get any further, just in case you're thinking, "She must have motherhood all figured out" (spoiler: I don't)—let me put you at ease by illuminating my humorous early motherhood story. Back then, in the pre-internet days of information over-load, I read every book stocked in the local library and foolishly believed I was totally prepared. Yet thirty minutes or so before my oldest was born, I loudly declared how I was *absolutely, one hundred percent, totally done* with labor, I couldn't handle it and I was quitting. Yes, quitting, despite the warming bassinet being ready and the staff prepping for delivery.

You know, in those last excruciatingly painful minutes of labor, I probably had a moment when I believed I would not survive. If I'm truthful, that was perhaps "moment one" of at least a thousand times when I didn't know how I would make it in my own motherhood story. My nurse stayed well past her shift to help a very stubborn first-time mom bring her child into the world. She took my tear-stained, cranky face in her hands and simply said, "You can't quit. You can do this." She could see beyond the moment.

She knew I wouldn't quit. And on that muggy June night, she

spoke universal truth to my fearful heart. She could see my grit tucked behind the fear. She could see my strength behind the doubt. She could see my love behind the pain. She just needed me to see my own strength.

Obviously, I didn't quit. My first child, Han, was born minutes later, and at the very moment that baby was put in my arms, a mom was born too.

Since I started writing to moms fifteen years ago, I'd like to think that in some small way, I am like that nurse who helped me see my own warrior-like strength. The notes have been written over the span of many years of mothering they are often written during one of my own unexpected or challenging, but otherwise normal, parenting moments. It's just a note to you saying, "You've got this. I can see beyond this moment. You, my friend, are not alone." I don't have all the answers. I've stumbled and fallen and stood up again, and again. I don't really write about the perfect stuff but rather the *figuring it out while in the middle of life* stuff. I share about the good, the bad, the ugly, and the abundance of moments called the in-betweens.

In case you're new to me, here's a bit of what I've shared and continue to share: divorce, the heartbreak of reconnecting with an estranged child, dealing with an autoimmune disease in my youngest, feeling overwhelmed with littles, living through financial crises, waiting up for teens, and simply being over-whelmed and overjoyed by the day in, day out demands of motherhood. I've also shared about my second marriage, co-par-enting, being a bonus (step) mom to four more amazing people, moving across the country, anxiety, and being an entrepreneur and coach.

I've shared how I've sat through many graduations: kindergarten, middle school, high school, college, and for my daughter in the military. I have sat in principal's offices, courtrooms, doctor's offices, bleachers, and car pick-up lines. I have sat on the floor next to beds, in counselor's rooms, in my chair, staring out the window, where I still often wonder what to do next and if I will make it through. Those places of sitting are pieces of each of our motherhood stories. They are places of hope, places of wonder, places of worry, and ultimately, places of showing up and showing love.

I've shared because I believe in the sharing; there is healing, there is power, and there is a reminder that the beauty of motherhood is often tucked in the corners where you and I sit and wonder, "Am I making a difference?" or, "Will the kids be OK?" or, "Am I the only one?" or, "Will I make it?" And yet, in it all, we gather our resolve, we try hard and we mother.

This book is a collection of motherhood reminder notes from me to you.

They are raw, unfiltered, and real.

They are about the messy and the beautiful.

They are about the ups, downs, and monotony of normal.

They are vulnerable and universal.

They are about moments of feeling alone, and being reminded you aren't as alone as you think.

They are the friend next to you, holding your hand and reminding you to breathe.

They are a celebration of motherhood, of your story.

They are encouragement from a friend who simply says, "You are mom enough."

Because in the end, on that first day of my motherhood story so long ago, we all need a reminder from another human to tell us we will make it.

We need to be seen. Noticed. Thanked. Loved. Appreciated. Cared for.

My friend, from me to you, wherever you are in your own motherhood story, hear these words, "You've got this."

From me, Rachel Marie Martin, writer of Finding Joy, who still has days where she wonders if she'll make it through yet, somehow, manages to make it. I want to say to all of you: I am proud of you because I know you will make it too.

One more thing, some of our family photos are sprinkled throughout this book. The photos I've shared are priceless glimpses into my motherhood story and I'm forever grateful to my family for allowing these images to be included.

How to use this book.

You don't have to read this book in order. You don't have to read all the letters at once. You can, but this book is designed to be that friend who gives you the hug of encouragement. Maybe you reread the same letter over and over, maybe you read a section, or maybe you read it all the way through. This book is designed to meet you right where you are in your own mother-hood story.

a good mom

A good mom has bad days & great days
normal days & overwhelming days
perfect days & trying days
supermom days & just being mom days
a whole lot of love &
real crazy motherhood days.

—Rachel Marie Martin
Findingjoy.net

section one

———

being a mom is enough

one

you are enough

I'm writing about simply being a mom.

There isn't much glamour. Think about it this way: It's about getting up in the morning, splashing your face with water, looking in the mirror, sighing, brushing your teeth (if you're lucky), picking up the toddler, wandering into the kitchen, pouring cereal in bowls, rinsing dishes, kissing the top of their heads, and waiting for your coffee to brew.

Minute by minute, until those hours add up to create a day, a week, a month, which turns into years, of you building a life while pouring into other little lives.

A beautiful life filled with ordinary mom moments.

Somehow, this world became filled with mixed messaging through social media. Perfection seems to be the expectation; women post things you should do and places you should go to follow your dreams, and the beauty of simply being a mother is completely lost.

Being a mom is enough.

Sometimes we want to look for big accomplishments and use them as a measure for success. We look at the cool science fair projects where our child could win the blue ribbon. But sometimes, we miss the hours of interacting with our kids. Holding glue sticks, doing research, and laughing as we discover exactly what we should make.

We want the trips to Disney, and we discount the time spent in the backyard. The measurement for success, joy, and happiness gets pushed so high by society's new norms that the little things—the mom-enough moments—are lost.

Do you know what matters? Conversations like this.

The other day my 15-year-old came to me and told me she missed me. Missed me? I couldn't believe it. I was completely caught off guard. I reminded her about the evenings we spent together at the movies, the trips to the yogurt bar, shopping at Forever 21, getting Starbucks, and all those cool mom things. She looked at me and told me that's not what she meant. She told me she wanted me present during the day.

Little things like stopping my crazy busy mom and work schedule to look at the graphic design she made on the computer, and I mean really looking at it while trying to appreciate her talents. It's about taking 30 minutes to play cards at the table with the kids and not checking email constantly on my phone. My email can wait 30 minutes. They cannot. It's about letting go and not worrying about the laundry and just being thankful I can do laundry for my family. Just being there. Cooking together. Laughing. Giving of myself in the simple things.

The things that don't get celebrated on Instagram or TikTok that much. "They're the *everyday mom things*." The things that most people probably will never see.

They don't see you stand in the bathroom and gather your resolve every morning or see those who mother alone without much support. They don't see all the back-and-forth trips to the car with bags of groceries. They don't see you counting to 10 a dozen times before noon so that you don't lose your mind. They don't see you look at the bank account and try to figure out how to make three meals with what's left in your pantry while you decide not to eat as much.

They don't see bandages placed on knees. Kisses on foreheads at night. Pillows pushed just the right way and blankets tucked perfectly. Tears that sting your eyes as you keep pushing through. Dinners prepped over the stove. Times of laughter over silly things. Hair brushed and pulled back into ponytails. Prayers over wandering teens. Prayers over little babes. Nights spent sleeping in a chair holding a sick child. Days where the house is a wreck but you're reading bedtime stories. The brave smile on your face when you're weary.

Those things matter.

Don't be weary, dear mother, in trying to keep up with a supermom agenda. That whole supermom who has everything together is just a misconception. There are real moms. Real, authentic moms who admit that they don't have it all together but keep on fighting. Scared and tired moms who keep fighting.

Moms who are overwhelmed by keeping up with littles all day long. Moms like you and me who sometimes feel lost in a world of unrealistic expectations.

A mother isn't based on external perfection.

A mother is a person, a woman, a fighter, a giver of self, just like you. She's the woman with little ones in her care whom she loves and sometimes wonders how she loves them because they're driving her batty, but she does. She fights, gives, prays, works, and doesn't give up even when she wants to throw in the elusive motherhood towel.

It is more than enough. You are amazing.

You can do this!

two

---

you can't quit, you've got this!

Don't quit.

I know it feels like the weight of the world is on your shoulders and that it really doesn't matter if the dishes are done or that no one really cares that you stayed up till two a.m. folding laundry or that sometimes you feel overlooked. I know there are moments when you sit in the car or on the bus or at your desk or behind the door in the bathroom and put your head in your hands while tears roll down your face. I know that sometimes you just want to throw in the towel and whisper (or scream) that you've had enough of this crazy world of mothering. I know.

I know because I have felt that way too.

I can remember sitting in the bathroom behind the door with my head in my hands thinking that I couldn't do this motherhood thing anymore and that I really didn't matter or make a difference and that I would never, ever catch up on laundry. (Why is laundry always a definer? And, just so you know, I've never ever caught up on laundry).

I remember hearing them fight over whose turn it was to play video games and all I could do was sit there and cry.

So, in all honesty, because I've been where you are, I'm writing now to remind you and to cheer you on by saying that even when you want to quit, you're still giving of yourself. As moms, we pull up on the bootstraps and try again. We do it over and over, and it matters more than you might ever realize in this moment.

Moms reach deep into places we never knew existed within us. The giving of ourself, and all that crazy, totally exhausting motherhood normal—matters.

There will be days that are hard. Weeks that are hard. Months that are hard.

Years that are hard.

Sometimes, sweet mother, life is just hard. But, even if it is difficult, it doesn't mean that we quit. Do you know why? You are brave, bold, powerful, mighty, and a warrior who happens to be fighting for yourself, your kids, and your family.

You can do this crazy, beautiful, and tiring motherhood thing.

I know you can.

You can pick yourself up, brush off the words that hold you back, and you can be mom enough today. You can look in your children's eyes and tell them how much you love them—even though you remember how much they sassed you this morning—and you still love them unconditionally. You can make those PB&J's and sliced apples for lunch today and can get the straw in the juice pouch on the first try. *Or the second*. You can drive those kids to soccer or ballet or school and tell yourself that you sitting in the car with them matters.

Quitting means stopping.

And you don't stop.

You can do this, sweet mother.

Motherhood doesn't look anything like I imagined when I was young. It doesn't look like those Pinterest boards full of birthday ideas with perfect fondant cakes and party favors that take three hours to make and cool glowing balloons that float in the pool. Yes, those moments are there sprinkled in the fabric of life. But seriously—now listen to me—those things don't make a mother. Those things, while beautiful, don't really matter in the life journey.

Do you know what matters? You. Right now, reading these words, who is about to give of herself for her family.

Do you realize what an amazing impact you are having?

Don't tell me about all the times you've messed up. I've got them as well. We all have messed up. That is simply part of life—trial and error and trying again. Do you remember all the times where you have done well? Or the times when you've been there? All the times when you sat behind the bathroom door with those tears and then stood up and tried again? We sit up at one a.m. rocking a toddler with a bad dream. Make dinner with toddlers crying and hanging on our legs. Give up something we need so that our child can get what he needs. Help with math. Read a story. Fold the clothes. Make lunches. Teach. Listen to their stories. Be silly. Laugh. Hold the puke bucket. Wipe faces. Put art on the wall. Watch them sleep.

We do all of those things and more and don't think twice about it.

Those are the moments in life that we are blessed to live.

So you may feel like you want to quit. Don't. Pick yourself up and tell yourself you can do this today. If you need to make a call for reinforcements just do it. It's always OK to ask for help.

You can.

You can for your family.

Don't look at how Sally is mothering, or what Facebook says, or how Instagram or Pinterest posts the picture of the perfect mother. You are the perfect mother for your children today.

Do not let the world qualify your motherhood. There is no price tag large enough that would ever illustrate the true value of motherhood. You are an amazing gift to your family.

I believe in you and all that you do.

Do you know why? Because your track record is 100 percent on those almost-quitting days.

What you are doing is not a small thing. It is a life-changing, life-nurturing, and life-growing real thing.

someday

Make today
your someday.
Take a chance.
Be brave.
Call a friend.
Forgive.
Start something new.
See the good.
Dare to dream.
Love.

—Rachel Marie Martin
Findingjoy.net

three

---

you matter

You, the enough mom right in the middle of motherhood. I want to remind you that what you are doing every single day matters.

Sure, you might nod your head and tell yourself it's *just* the dishes or *just* picking up toys, or *just* anything. I've done that—that dismissing of all of those many things that moms do. In fact, I do that all too often. I dismiss all the ins and outs of the day and simply brush it off as just another day. I'll tell myself that this is *just* what happens and what we do as mothers—this giving of self over and over—and all the nitty-gritty stuff doesn't really matter. It's easy to lose sight of it all as you get lost in the monotony of the everyday.

And more than that—being a mother and all that you do every single day makes a difference. A huge difference. These are lives that you are changing. Real lives who look to you for love, wisdom, support, and comfort. Those children need you.

All those things—diaper changes, driving to taekwondo, sleeping on a hard floor next to a toddler who had a bad dream, wiping spaghetti-covered faces, talking about not eating too much sugar, helping with science facts, pumping bike tires, reading books again and again, memorizing math facts, cleaning up the backyard, laughing when you feel like crying—all that stuff matters.

You could just keep saying that it's *just what a mom does,* and not look at the impact, the value, that mothers truly have on lives. But today, I encourage you to embrace how much all that real life motherhood stuff that you do every day makes an impact. Look with fresh eyes—eyes that are giving yourself grace—at that list of things you do, knowing that despite the ups and downs and ins and outs and good days and bad days, what you are doing really makes a difference.

What you are doing is not a small thing.

These are the things that matter—when you're in your last days you'll remember this. Your children will remember as well. They will remember that mom was there for me through the good and the bad.

It's OK to go back to all you are doing—cleaning, working, driving, cheek-wiping, baking, clothes-folding, everyday normal motherhood things—and hold your head high.

More than having the perfect house, the perfect body, the perfect schedule, the perfect kids, the perfect anything, you are a game changer. A life changer. You are their mother.

Being a mother is a beautiful thing.

do your best

With your stumbles
and your triumphs.
With your tears
and your laughter.
With your giving
and your loving
and your showing up.
Because no one does
your best better
than you.

—Rachel Marie Martin
Findingjoy.net

four

sweet anxious mom

It is OK.

You might not even know why you are anxious. You might worry that you are dropping the ball with your kids. You might be wondering what is wrong with you. You might feel like you're failing.

Those feelings. They are just there. I don't know why you wake at one a.m. with your heart racing, but I know it is hard. I know you feel alone.

I also know that you've forgotten a bit.

And that is why I am writing to you right now. To remind you. To give you perspective, a bit of a place to land for your heart. So listen, you are so important. Those kids who drive you crazy need you. They love you. They don't really care that sometimes you don't make creative dinners or that you got stressed out over homework. They care about you. Waking up every single day for them. Of course, they'll never articulate that to you, but trust me, it matters.

If it didn't, they wouldn't watch for you out of the bus window as it drives by the house to their stop. They wouldn't wave when they see you walking out the door. They wouldn't care. But they do. They show it in the way kids do. And most of the time it's so seemingly ungrateful. But sometimes those ways are the ways they show you love and how you are needed.

And there is nothing wrong with you. Can you just listen to me? Just for a moment. You are OK, for real. We weren't meant to live numb to this world. And sometimes that means you have moments of sadness mixed with moments of joy. It's a balance. So don't cut yourself down when you're in the moments of the bottom of a wave. That's right, that's what I want you to remember: emotions are like a wave, and sometimes you are joyful and sometimes neutral and sometimes sad, but they come and go and ebb and flow.

You aren't defined by them, sweet soul.

So you have a bad day. You have many good days as well.

So you messed up. You have many times where you kicked ass.

So you got teary. You have many moments where you laugh.

So you were overwhelmed. You have many moments where you are in control.

So you felt alone. You have many moments where you are amid friends.

You see, during those anxious moments, you don't remember the second part of the story. You see all the holes in the boat and not that the boat is moving. I need you to look up. I need you to remember that you were created with great power, strength, and vision. I need you to take care of that heart.

And I need you to love you for you.

Yes, that.

Maybe you forgot about the importance of loving you for who you are, but trust me, it's critical. You'd never tell you children to not love themselves. The same goes for you. Give yourself a break and a lot of grace. Brush off those doubts.

You are one amazing person. You are worth fighting for.

It's time to remember that again.

Fight for you. Stop letting all the reasons that things will never change—or you don't matter or you are stuck—define your tomorrow. Sorry that it seems so hard, but listen: I care about you. Yes, you. You who does amazing things but has had a moment where the pressure of life has clouded your perspective of awesomeness. Anxiousness will pass. I promise you. I made it through.

You are a brave soul.

You are not alone. I believe in you. In your story.

I truly do.

Can I dare you to share this with a friend? With someone who might also be feeling anxious? To let her know that she, too, is *not* alone? Together we can change the world and bring hope.

breathe

Your kids need you.
Not perfect. Just you.
With your worries.
Your laughs.
Your fails.
And your try agains.
Your love.
Your showing up.
That's what matters.
Breathe, sweet mom.

—Rachel Marie Martin
Findingjoy.net

section two

———

discouraging days

five

---

you are not failing

You're not.

If you and I were sitting in Starbucks and you had your fave drink and I had my caramel macchiato, I'd look at you and I'd tell you the truth: you're not failing.

I know. I'm guessing you'd wipe away the tears and look up and try to nod your head, but inside you'd think that those are nice words but seriously she has no idea. You know why I know? Because I've sat in a coffee shop across from a friend, a friend who looked me smack in the face and told me that I wasn't failing and that I was instead doing a great job.

I wanted to tell her about the dishes from yesterday sitting on my counter. And how the pile of storybooks wasn't read again. And that I'm a week behind in laundry. And that I got really irritated at the mixture of 13 toys all dumped in a pile that two days ago was sorted into 13 labeled boxes. I wondered if she knew that, some days, I get up and just go through the mom motions without finding much joy.

It felt like dull menial work.

How could she tell me I wasn't failing?

Somehow in the mixed-up world of media we are bombarded with picture perfect moms. Society doesn't give us a break. Once the *New*

York Times published an article about the intense pressure on moms to look a certain way—also known as perfect—after they give birth. And then? Then we're to be ultra-creative, crafty, humorous, happy, chipper, up before dawn, to sleep after dark, with our sinks shined, the laundry folded, tomorrow's breakfast in the crockpot and tomorrow's dinner—pulled from our once-a-month cooking—thawing in the fridge while we work out for 20 minutes on odd days and 40 minutes on even days, with hair always done, makeup ready, fridge stocked, craft closet bursting with ideas for that perfect afternoon art project that we'll place on our recycled wood and Mod Podge-adorned hand-painted chalkboard. And we're smiling.

But it's eight a.m. and we're just getting up. The baby was up all night or the toddler sick or, honestly, we're just tired. We get our coffee and flip on Facebook and our stream is flooded with stuff people have already done and we're racing to catch up with this perfect, never-feel-like-you're-failing mom ideal.

You know what my friend told me? She told me to slow down. Slow down? How in the world when I felt like I was failing was I to slow down? I had way too much to do and I needed to read that parenting book to work on my attitude and ... and ... and. And she told me, "Enough." And that I was a good mom.

You know, you're not failing.

You need to start to see all you do accomplish in a day. All the smiles of encouragement, meals made, clothes changed, books read, and more. We're out of breath, racing, and exhausted, but truly not failing. Failing means stopping. Not getting up, not trying, not giving. That's not you.

I want you to stop telling yourself you're failing. Instead, I want you to replace it with these four words: *"I can do this."*

You can do this.

Those soundtrack words and feeling about failing are just feelings. Don't let them define you anymore. If you hear, *"I'm failing,"* replace it immediately with, *"I can do this."*

If you were across the table from me, that is what I would tell you.

And, of course, I'd tell you to do one thing and do it well.

I'm going to write and say it again and again: Write your list of things you want to do, need to do, and would love to do today with your family. And then, do one thing from each list. If you stumble, brush yourself off and start again. Don't worry that the neighbor across the street seems to be doing 20 or the Pinterest pin tells you that the perfect home can be achieved in Six Easy Steps. This is your life. You are the perfect mother for those children. God knew when He blessed those kids to you.

Remember that.

You are a good mom.

You can do this. One step, one day, at a time.

six

---

it's ok to feel discouraged sometimes

If you're sitting there, on your side of this book reading these words, and your heart is feeling heavy and discouraged, I am sorry. Sometimes life, the to-do lists, the daily grind, the challenges, the normal, the ups and downs, and all of that has a way of pulling all the energy from us. All that's left is a massive and uncomfortable pile of discouragement.

I remember watching movies, those fairy tale and Disney specials, when I was little. Even in intense conflicts, everything seemed to resolve beautifully by the end. Real life can't be wrapped up in a two-hour show. Life oftentimes can simply feel ridiculously hard. Do you know what? I hate that perhaps you are reading these simple words and thinking, *You have no idea how discouraged I feel.*

I wrote the earlier letter about feeling like you're failing because I've felt that way before. And now, today, I am writing this one because I, too, have felt discouraged. We all have different stories—yours and mine and others—and yet we all at some level can understand the angst of discouragement.

It sits there. You watch others, looking at their lives, and wonder why yours isn't the same. Then the questions rattle through our brains: *Why me? Why not? How come? Don't I deserve better?*

You need hope. A goal. A reminder.

You need to remember that life can be beautiful in the middle of normal. You need to remember that you matter and that your heart and your dreams matter. Remember that motherhood and parenthood changes lives. You need to remember that normal can be wonderful, and even though some days it feels like you do the same thing day after day after day, those same things build on each other and create this thing called real life.

You need to remember how important you are.

Yes, you. Right there, right now, with tears in your eyes. In fact, I have tears writing this because as I write to you I write to me, and oftentimes my heart is also weary.

Just yesterday, I picked up the same toys that I had sorted the day before and I resorted them, I figured out a miracle for dinner that didn't involve everything coming from a box. I cleaned the kitchen and shined the sink, straightened the towels, folded laundry, and then went to bed thinking I had everything perfect. I was ready for the next day where I would triumph as a mom.

Oh yeah, I was ready.

Then reality set in.

The perfectly clean house got messy before the breakfast dishes were done, the amazing Food Network dinner option that everyone raved about online was a disaster, the laundry basket with neatly precise folded clothes was dumped out, I didn't get my shower and someone came over, water spilled everywhere, and the new markers were left out without caps and bled on the couch. Oh yes, and there were late bills to pay with money that wasn't there and relationships that were strained. And you know what? I ended up discouraged. Really discouraged.

It's easy to feel that way when life hits hard.

It's easy to feel that way when life seems to be on a repeat cycle of discouraging moments.

But truthfully, I don't want to live discouraged, and I really don't want you to live feeling discouraged. I read your sweet notes—your emails and comments and Facebook posts—and I read about how you want to live this life of intentionality, embracing and loving the little things. I love that you and I are a generation of women who are looking to rise above the circumstances and are willing to reclaim motherhood as a noble job beyond the perfection-driven ideal that runs rampant. When you and I look at each other and tell each other *"well done," "you matter,"* and *"you are making a difference,"* we are kicking discouragement out the door.

So today, I am looking at you and telling you those words:

Well done. You matter. And you are making a difference.

Because that is truth.

Rise up, discouraged mom. Pull your hair back. Kiss those kids. And continue.

seven

all moms worry

All mothers worry about being a good mom. You worry if you're doing enough or if your kids love you or if you really have this mother thing figured out or if your kids should do more or less or if you spend enough time with them. You just worry.

Well, guess what? I do too—I think it's just part of the amazing journey of mothering. I'm not going to write you a letter telling you to stop wanting to be a good mom. In fact, I think it's beautiful that you and I want to be good moms. Could you imagine the opposite? Not caring? Not wanting to be good for our kids or not wanting to learn or change?

No. Longing to be a good mom is a good thing. Savor that, cultivate it, and do not run from it.

It's easy to confuse worry with wants and things that you think you need to do.

Mothers are truly brave, but it's easy to worry about whether our mothering skills measure up to the societal norms (whatever that means). Those norms could include eating organic, not eating fast food, kids on the honor roll, educational choices, reading by an early age, awesome living room that looks like it was designed by Joanna Gaines. All those things by themselves can be good, but hear me when I say: those things do not define whether you are a good mom.

Motherhood isn't defined by where you shop for groceries, what brand of clothes your child wears, or when you send out those late Christmas cards. It is not defined by the latest parenting books or parenting podcast. Those parameters have no weight on the good motherhood scale.

Being a good mom isn't about doing. It's about being.

Being the cheerleader. Being the fighter for them when no one seems to be listening. Being the one who gives of herself even when there is not much left to give. Being there in the middle of the night or being the one who listens. Being there sitting in the car waiting for them to emerge from their class. Being the one who helps them pick out the right shirt. Being the one who's mastered the art of counting to 10 many times to avoid losing control. Being the one who cooks lunches that no one likes but you smile anyway. Being the one who wants to be a good mom and keeps trying every single day.

It is a beautiful thing, my friends, to want to be a good mom.

It means you care, you love, and you are invested in those blessings—the only ones in the world to call you *mom*. I know it's tough. Our world screams that you should be doing so many things in the middle of this seems-like-forever-but-really-happens-in-the-blink-of-an-eye mothering journey.

They need you—more than the next program, the next class, the latest clothes, and the coolest apps. Remember those things? They are good. But they do not define good moms. The bottom line is that they need your lap to sit in at the end of the day. They need you to brush away the tears and to tell them how much they matter. They need you to be there for them and to love them without conditions.

You see you have a gift—and that gift in being a good mom is to be the one who cultivates the truth in your child's heart about how important they are and how valuable their dreams are and how much they matter.

You are a good mom.

Don't let things that are unimportant rob you of that. Sure, it is OK to learn from all the amazing resources and voices out there. But remember: if all of the media and its information was stripped away and it was just you and the kids, you would still be there. That is what truly matters—it's you being there, investing in their lives, teaching them truth, and simply loving them. It's about showing up.

Be there and embrace today.

Take your photos, laugh, and celebrate the true gift of motherhood.

And let go of that mom worry.

eight

---

stuck in a rut

Sometimes it feels like the same thing day after day.

Repeat. And repeat again. And again.

You get up, not on your own time, and you start giving from the beginning of the day until your weary head hits the pillow late at night. The list of to-dos is longer than the hours in the day, and it feels as if you're adding more to it than you are crossing off. After a while, the days start to blur together into one long stuck-in-a-rut cycle. Instead of going to bed feeling rewarded, fulfilled, and energized, you go to bed wondering if you'll have enough energy to make it through another day of the same thing.

Have you wondered if mothering was supposed to be this way? I thought it was about sweet morning hugs, and Gymboree clothes, and organic waffles with berries and hand-whipped cream in the morning. And I dreamed of a clean house with a trendy Pottery Barn decor, a stocked pantry, and gourmet four-cheese macaroni.

But it's not like that most days, and we end up feeling stuck.

Where did the creativity go? The energy? The longing for those perfect motherhood days we dreamed about when we were young.

You're a good mom even on those feeling-stuck-in-a-rut days of motherhood.

Let me tell you, having a bad day, or feeling stuck or irritated or without creativity, doesn't mean that you're not a good mom. We all go through those days when we just don't want to do one more load of laundry *and* we tell everyone not to put anything in the hamper for at least 20 minutes. *And* we're tired of tacos for dinner *and* we just want the living room to stay clean until 8:45a.m. Having a stuck-in-a-rut day doesn't mean that you're not doing a great job.

You're just stuck in a rut.

Too often we look at the big things to change the pattern. We think that if we had a teeny bit more money or free time or the latest book, or if we lost weight or ate better or started to run or read the next best parenting book, we might get out of this rut and be able to change our mindset.

Who wants to live overwhelmed? We want to be happy, right? But to me, happiness is elusive. You can chase it—and it lasts just for a moment—and then it's gone. And then you're left right where you started.

Joy doesn't mean happy. Joy is a posture of the heart that embraces the present in the ups and downs and seeks gratitude in the everyday.

I want you to seek joy and find joy, instead.

We all have those days of feeling stuck in a rut—it's OK. If there were such a thing as supermom, she would eventually get stuck in a rut as well.

Moms, start by taking a peek at your day. Chances are, some things feel overwhelming and are making the day unusually hard. Identify them. Choose one or two and change it up. Start with your children. Alter the routine: make pancakes for breakfast, go play in the backyard, pull out the crayons and color. Be engaged. Then look for one thing in your home: laundry, cooking, cleaning, or emails? Work to change that one thing. Develop a system for laundry, or some new menus, or a strategy for email.

Just don't sit in the rut. The longer you stay stuck, the harder it is to get out of it.

I've discovered that I could spend so much time sitting in the rut moments or the overwhelmed moments of life that I don't move. So today, I want you to move. Be intentional—take five minutes and look at your day and what you can do to change it. The change comes from you—not from the externals, but from you.

You can do it.

You are a mother with creativity, energy, and joy. Sometimes you lose it for a bit, but it's still there tucked inside of you. When you go to bed tonight, write down or take a mental note—or write in lipstick on the mirror, in email, or on Facebook—at least three good things from today.

Three things.

That's it. Work on your one thing to change or do differently, and then record three moments of the good stuff. Three moments of joy.

You will keep moving forward.

So, dear mom who feels stuck, let's get moving and get out of that rut.

One step forward. One step. Then another.

You can do it. Ready?

Let's go.

perfect mom

My kids don't have a perfect mom.
They have me.
Imperfect.
But I try, boy, do I try.
Sometimes it feels too small, not
enough, like I'm letting them down.
Sometimes I have no clue what to do
but I will still show up, stand there
and cheer them on. Loudly.
Maybe I'm not perfect, maybe they
don't get everything, maybe life has
good and bad days and a whole bunch
of normal. But that's okay.
I taught them to be real. To show up.
That it is good to proudly support
those you love. That family is about
being together. And that the best gift
of all is, in fact, love. Perfection is overrated.

—Rachel Marie Martin
Findingjoy.net

section three

———

letting go of perfect

nine

---

perfection

I'm the gal who sorts markers, pencils, crayons, and scissors into separate labeled boxes. I like the books in order and the movies by category and clothes hung in colored sequence depending on season and sleeve length. I like the day to go like clockwork, with check marks, goals completed, and not many bumps in the wished-for smooth road. I don't care for messes, and I have a hard time getting things done when there's clutter.

A perfectionist, right? And, yet, as I've written so many times, I'm the perfectionist who tries so hard not to be the perfectionist.

Life is messy.

Real life doesn't really care if I have the craft supplies sorted or that the island is clean or that the clothes are folded and put away perfectly. Real life is like my Christmas tree one year, with its carefully decorated and ornament-full bottom and the perfect topper I'd fussed over. And guess what? It fell over within one hour of completion. Yes, one hour. Ornaments, water, lights, and all, in a tangled mess scattered all over my floor in a giant glitter ball with shards of glass and tinsel— this was my not-so-perfect result.

And in the moment that it fell, I was running late.

I had a dinner to go to, I was straightening my hair, and all of the sudden I was faced with a giant pine tree and garland curveball in the routine. Our seven-and-a-half-foot tree, heavy with ornaments, rested on my area rug in the living room with piles of Hungarian gold glass bulbs that I had so carefully picked out from the clearance rack at Pier One, now crushed underneath.

Laugh or cry?

I chose to laugh. The perfectionist who tries hard not to be such a perfectionist, in the moment just laughed. My family was watching—waiting to see my response—and they mattered more than the bulbs scattered everywhere. Then I saw my daughter Grace's first year Christmas 2001 ornament—a little bear on a pastel rocking chair—snapped in two. As I picked it up, my oldest daughters, who both stepped in to help me clean, looked at me and said, "It's just a thing, Mom."

Just a thing.

My perfectionist heart had to let it go. It was just a thing and they mattered more. They watched me as I looked at them and told them, "Yes, it's just a thing, you're right."

So to you, the mom who might like everything perfect or who is living in a life where nothing seems to make sense, I'm telling you that you are not alone in this world of perfectionism. Despite the Hallmark movies, the perfect Target toy ads, and the Currier and Ives decorations at the store, life is simply messy. Honestly, some of the hardest years of my life have happened around Christmas. I don't know if it is the expectation placed around the holidays, so that then when things go awry they feel even more painful and difficult. It feels that way. So for one who likes stuff perfect, that makes this season of hypothetical perfectness even harder.

But, mom—you can do this in a not-so-perfect life.

Do you know why I think I love everything so perfect?

It's about me trying to control my circumstances.

But I'm learning, as was perfectly illustrated with my tree falling on that snowy night, that there are things that we can't control: health, finances, relationships, trees falling, kids fussing, snow days when you had plans to go out. And in those moments we just have to let go of things and choose to embrace relationships. Even when things are messy, there can still be beauty. That tree that fell was standing the next morning despite ornaments that needed to be rearranged and lights that needed restringing. The point wasn't that it was perfect. The point was that it was standing.

Dear mom, whose life might not be perfect, remember that life can still be good. You are still standing.

You and I and all the other moms out there who love to keep stuff a certain way have a challenge. That challenge? To embrace today and not let perfectionist ideals define our happiness. You can still be joyful, creative, encouraging, content, motivated, loving, caring, hopeful, happy, determined, and full of life even when life isn't perfect.

Look at your kids. They want you just as you are. They want you to be there in the trenches laughing with them and ignoring the crayons and markers that are mixed in a pile on the table and instead looking at them and giving them a real, joyful smile. That matters the most.

Motherhood is an amazing journey of learning to let go and embracing chaos and living with a heart that is content in the middle of crazy.

Your children need you. Not the perfect mom, but you. That is grace.

Now go. Live today. Expect it won't be perfect, but still embrace the beauty in today.

ten

you are not alone

You are not alone when you push the snooze button and wish for five more minutes of sleep and push the snooze button again and then proceed to roll out of bed ten minutes later than you should and start the day racing out of breath just a bit.

You are not alone if you find yourself repeating, *No, you may not do that* and, *Stop that* and, *Seriously? We've established that rule* and, *No more media* and, *Stop picking on your brother (or sister)* every day.

You are not alone if sometimes you look at the Facebook stream and think that your life doesn't measure up to the highlight stream being culled over there.

You are not alone if sometimes you stand in the kitchen and have no clue what to make for dinner and then you find yourself breathing a sigh of relief for the chicken nuggets in the freezer and can of corn in the cupboard.

You are not alone if you sit at the table and struggle with fifth grade math and have to google the answer to finding the mean, median, and mode again.

You are not alone if you don't coupon. Or if you do coupon.

You are not alone if your kids play on electronics and then you feel guilty because you let them play just a bit longer so you could get one more thing done.

You are not alone if you've doubted that what you're doing as a mother really matters and you've stood in the bathroom and looked in the mirror and wondered if you're enough.

You are not alone if you're tired. Trust me, you're really not alone here.

You are not alone if you've ever felt alone in this motherhood journey.

You are not alone if you have that moment in the beginning of the day when you ponder how today will go and if you'll get the to-do list done and if there is enough coffee in the cabinet to sustain you.

You are not alone if you work. Or if you stay at home. Or if you do both.

You are not alone if you feel guilt for working. Or staying at home. Or for both.

You are not alone if you've saved Pinterest boards full of awesome-ness and you've only created two. Or maybe three. Or if they're full of motivational quotes on motherhood and life like mine is.

You are not alone if you have laundry to fold and a kitchen to clean but instead you decide to close your eyes just for a moment.

You are not alone when you love your kids like crazy and can pick them out of the crowd of thirty-eight kids waiting at the curb for you to pick them up from school.

You are not alone if you know all the songs from Frozen and will belt them along with your preschooler.

You are not alone for finding joy in having a kitchen counter that is clean or that the laundry is done or that there is nothing on your calendar for today.

You are not alone in worrying that you are doing enough for your children even though deep down you truly really are and yet you have those pesky doubts that like to remind you of all the times you've stumbled instead of seeing where you soared.

You are not alone in wanting friendships.

You are not alone if your child is the one at Target having the meltdown at the register because you refuse to purchase the toy conveniently placed at eye level.

You are not alone when you consider going to Target or the grocery store by yourself a mini vacation.

You are not alone if you've ever struggled with mom guilt or comparison or feeling like you're the only one who doesn't have the ideal life.

You are not alone in having dishes that need to be done or a bathroom that needs to be cleaned or any of those normal house chores that we often don't give ourselves grace to realize that we're always in the middle of them and they're never ever done.

You are not alone in wishing your home looked a certain way even though you have kids and that means that there are handprints on the walls, marker stains on the table, mismatched socks in the laundry room, and a bunch of stuff that always needs to be sorted.

You are not alone if you've stayed up all night with a sick little one and taken temperatures and grabbed the Tylenol and had to decide if you go to the doctor or not and back and forth.

You are not alone in having days that don't go perfectly.

You are not alone when you have wonderful days that simply make you smile.

You are not alone when you walk in their rooms at night to look at those sleeping faces and you wonder why in the world they pushed all of your buttons two hours earlier.

You are not alone if you go to bed tired and you don't remember your head hitting the pillow.

You are not alone when you realize what a gift motherhood is in those times where you can slow down enough to catch your breath.

You are not alone if you just sigh when you look at all you've done, and you see the beauty in the very extraordinary ordinary.

You are not alone, dear mother.

You are not alone in this crazy journey called motherhood.

You are not alone.

You are instead strong, beautiful, powerful, amazing, and a life changer.

Sometimes we all need a reminder of all that we are: Motherhood. Collective.

And that we are not alone.

see the good

We live in a
world
where it is easy
to be offended.
But what happens if
we decide to
see the good first?
To give the benefit of the
doubt?
To respond in love?
Life happens in a second.
Live it seeing the good.
First.

—Rachel Marie Martin
Findingjoy.net

eleven

keep showing up

My son dropped his phone, but he didn't realize it until we drove to the middle school for a concert. I sat in the car trying to mull over what to do—risk going back on snowy slippery roads or hope we'd find it in an hour. We stayed.

The inches of snow made that phone impossible to find when we returned. But let me tell you—I tried. I was the mom with a rusty green metal rake raking her snow-covered yard. I was the mom kicking every inch of snow with my feet. I was the mom out there for twenty minutes more while everyone else went inside to warm up.

That's just what we do as moms.

We show up. We put ourselves out there.

We do crazy things like attempting to find white Samsung phones in thick, wet, last-day-of-November snow.

We make countdown chains and sprinkle glitter and bake cookies thinking that this year we'll stay happy throughout the process. And when the flour gets everywhere we lose it just a bit and wish for the clean kitchen.

We fold shirts knowing that they will be pulled from the drawers and thrown on the ground, to be followed by, "I have nothing to wear."

We stop our kids from fighting over things that drive us crazy.

The other day while the kids were in school, I climbed a tree to put white twinkling lights in it. I did it for them. The other week I drove my six-year-old to Children's Hospital Minnesota for lab work. I did it for him. The other night I stayed awake with my eight-year-old when he had a bad dream. I did so because I love him.

Chances are you have these little things that you do too.

Chances are you could write your own list of all these simple things that got lost in the fabric of the busy that you do every day for your family. And you do it without looking for gold stars or *that's awesome* or any of it. Chances are most of it simply fades into the timeline of your life. Chances are you are probably thinking that you haven't done enough or that you're messing up your kids. Or you're kicking yourself for responding too short. Or you're just feeling overwhelmed. Or stuck. Or like you're failing.

But chances are that you, just like me, have done some pretty profound motherhood things. Ordinary things.

And sometimes those ordinary things take so much work. They take us counting to ten one hundred times. They take us trying to not get super frustrated over geography projects that just feel like a waste of time. They take us picking up toys again and again and again. Sometimes we get so frustrated about picking up toys that we throw them all in a bag to throw away and then find ourselves picking out favorites because we love them.

Chances are you have a whole bunch of ordinary things *that add up to life*. Things that you could share, if only you wouldn't dismiss them. If only you wouldn't attach "just" to them. If only you wouldn't think that it's no big deal. If only you would let the tears fall when they need to. If only you would start to see again just how beautiful and extraordinary and wonderful a person you are.

Life has a tendency to throw us curve balls. It can suck the wind from us and make us weep at night. It can make us feel like we'll never measure up. It can hide us from seeing how powerful and brave we are to do those simple things.

Like notes in the lunch boxes. Sitting in the school pick-up line. Making a favorite dinner. Drying the winter gear when they come in. Again and again. Rolling snowballs. Laughing when they laugh. Rocking babies. Taking temperatures. Reading books and skipping parts. Teaching how to put snow pants over boots. Brushing hair. Wiping tables. Going to bed exhausted. Waking tired. Loving when we don't even know how.

We're all flawed. I'm not perfect, you're not perfect, and our kids aren't perfect.

So tonight, today, or whenever you're reading this—you deserve to see you the way the rest of us see you.

A mom that shows up.

Day after day. Night after night. Good day after good day. Hard day after hard day. Ordinary day, normal day, just a day. Loving your kids.

That, my friends, is what matters.

So before you close this book and move on with your life, I want you to take a breath, look at the hands in front of you, and be over-whelmed with wonder for all that you do. Those hands love. They button coats. They give. They wipe away tears. They write notes. They hold hands in them until those hands grow. They mother.

Carry on. You are brave even when you feel small.

Thank you for showing up.

twelve

mom guilt

Mom guilt can eat at the core of our mothering heart.

How often do you lie in bed at night thinking feeling guilty for all the things you didn't get done during the day or the stories you didn't read or the fact that your kids ate chips instead of the organic baby-sized carrots with the dipping sauce? Or you worry that your five-year-old had too much screen time that day when, instead, you should have been making a truly cool craft with glitter and super sticky glue?

And let's not even start on all the other stuff like work, school, and other activities. And there is that pesky but oh-so-loved social media mom who has a million and four fabulous ideas for you and your kids. But instead, you search through social media for a community of real mothers who don't have time to do everything.

Mom guilt is real.

Yeah, I know, I deal with it.

It's that voice constantly telling you that you're not good enough. It's the "should have" moments that negate all the other moments when you gave more than you had to give.

Please do not sit in mom guilt.

I don't want you to spend another moment sitting in past disappointments. No more. Do you make mistakes? Absolutely. I do too. Every single day I can name something I wish I had done better. That is part of life, part of being real, but remember, perfectionism kills contentment.

Sitting in mistakes means missing out on today.

Do not sit in those past moments. Mothers, right now, you are being given a gift. As cliché as it sounds, true life truly *is* a gift. Each moment you have with your children is an amazing gift. You can't allow guilt from yesterday to lessen the good that can happen today.

This applies to right now, this moment, as you read these words. You know what? Maybe you were having a hard day and needed a break, so you let your children watch Nick Junior so that you could call a friend or make coffee or play solitaire on the computer.

That is OK. Sometimes motherhood is about simply making it through a day. I know, we don't talk about that, but it's true. If you need to deal with a hard day, then deal with it and do what you need to do to get through.

No guilt.

Just don't sit in it. I'm telling you: pick up where you left off and start again. That's the thing about guilt—when it's allowed to fester and brew, it is simply difficult to start again. Release it. Let it go. Those are also words of mine this year. Let it go—learn from those thoughts about what you wish you had done, but instead of letting them define you today, use them as motivation to do the things you wish you had done.

Read a novel. Color in the coloring book. Listen to music with your teens. Pick up the kids from class and hug them. Make dinner. Let go of the guilt and know that you are doing your best. Be involved. Be present in the today.

Mom guilt can hold us back. Kick that guilt to the curb! So often it's just our own thoughts that freeze us or the ideas we get in our heads about what others do, or our guilt springs from an idea of what we think is normal. No mom is perfect—you've heard this many times. We all, at some time, deal with the idea that we're not measuring up.

Yet there is no ruler, no bar, no perfect mother. There is the real mom.

The mom who wishes she had not snapped about that box of Legos dumped on the living room floor or the spilled milk—and then that mom picks up the Legos, wipes up the milk, and still looks her kids in the eyes and tells them she loves them. The mom who works really hard, comes home, starts the laundry, and still reads stories at bedtime. The mom who is up half the night with a crying baby and who ran out of coffee in the morning but still manages to smile and hug on the kids.

I bet that sounds like you, but sometimes it's easy to forget to see all the good. Try focusing on the times where you did well. You do that for your kids, and now it is time to love *yourself* enough to give yourself grace.

No guilt.

Empowerment. That's my word for you. When those guilty thoughts fill your mind—wishing for what you *could* have done—think instead about things you *can* do, *want* to do, and let the rest go.

Now go. Be a mom today. No more guilt.

simply mom

Today in an auditorium
full of parents
my son scanned the room
looking for me.
When he saw me his
face lit up the room.
He wasn't looking for
the perfect parent.
He was looking for his mom.
Don't ever forget the power
of simply being their mom.

—Rachel Marie Martin
Findingjoy.net

section four

———

life is short

thirteen

___

"in a minute"

I just told him: "in a minute."

It was this book, an old Arthur book from my older daughters, and my six-year-old wanted me to read it to him. Caleb had asked twice already during the day and again last night when I was making dinner. But I was truly busy—I had ballet schedules to keep, dinner to make, a board meeting to attend, a review to write, and an email to respond to that was supposed to have been done yesterday.

"In a minute, Caleb."

I kept moving. Working on my long list of to-dos. The book? It just sat there on the old plaid couch on a stack of books waiting to be read. The next morning, I sat down with a piping hot mug of coffee and my laptop and a quiet house so I could work. I looked over at the well-worn book and thought of that six-year-old sleeping upstairs, waiting for the "in a minute" to come.

The book-reading minute never came yesterday.

I know you are busy. I get that frenzied and unending pace of things to do.

We're constantly pushed to do more, create more, cook more, bake more, decorate more, teach more, organize more, garden more, host more, volunteer more, drive more, and excel more. And ultimately, we compare more. Moms will see that massive to-do list, the never-ending tasks, the laundry spilling into the hallway, and the toys dumped out. No wonder we say "in a minute."

For me it means stopping.

It means stepping off the frenzied to-do list and sitting. It means hanging up the phone or closing the laptop and choosing to get down on their level, whatever level it may be, and looking them in the eye and listening to the questions that so often get the quick "in a minute" answers. Not the kind of listen where have to cry, trying to get the distracted me to pay attention and listen.

It's hard.

Being a mother often feels like living in a gigantic game of catch-up. You get everything just so, just perfect, and then, well, then someone puts socks in the laundry hamper or the orange juice spills or the phone rings or the timer on the oven buzzes. Real stuff. Keeps us busy. All the time.

Don't let life—the crazy pace of life, the unending cycle of busy—rob you from the minutes with your family. Don't let the books that they want to read stay on the couch for days until the six-year-old has grown and lost interest in the story.

Just watch every "in a minute."

Or each "just a second," "wait," "hold on," and more. Does it mean never using those phrases? Absolutely not.

I mean, seriously, if you're changing a diaper and your four-year-old wants to go outside and the six-year-old is asking for paints, and the eight-year-old wants to go on a bike ride, there is no way you can do it all right at that second. However, you can give an intentional, answer: "We can bike this afternoon," "We will go outside after lunch," or "We can't do that today."

It's the real answer that matters (and sometimes it means saying no). It's not about dropping everything all the time—although some of the time we simply do need to let our agenda go—instead it's about watching the answers so that the real important things don't get left sitting on a couch for days.

It's progress. Not perfection.

Today I'm reminding you, the "in a minute" mom, to remember those words of truth. Just keep trying, working to do those "in a minute" things that matter.

You really are doing a great job. It's progress.

Just pick up the book and read it now. That's exactly what I did.

fourteen

vacuuming is beautiful

My older boys' bedroom looked like it had never been cleaned before: toys mixed with peels of a clementine, pens and markers, clothes, dirty socks, books, and anything else you could imagine. It was all there percolating into this gigantic mess that took me four hours to straighten. Left over from weeks when the cleaning was superficial, and this was the obvious result. It made me very grumbly.

Grumble, grumble, grumble.

The boys came in and offered to help and I just snapped at them. "I don't need your help. If you had just managed your room better, this crazy chaos wouldn't have happened. I'll just do it myself." Martyr mom. Complaining, not accepting help, just grumbling my way through normal.

I pulled out the vacuum, determined to at least get the floor clean even though I had a massive pile of things to sort through. I flipped it on and the soft hum filled the room. Then I looked up to see Caleb sitting on his bed, stacking books and pulling Legos out of the pile and tossing them in the large bin. He looked at me, the frustrated mom, and simply smiled. A sincere I-love-you-even-when-you-complain-about-this-messy-room smile.

As I held the vacuum, still running, my eyes welled up with tears.

When did I lose the beauty in this normal, even though the normal like today was frustrating? When did the gift of having children in my home get lost and I instead just wanted every little thing perfect and without mess?

Childhood is messy.

My goodness, life is messy.

We don't know how our days will play out. This became even more important to me as I looked at pictures of children whose lives were unfairly lost in reckless school shootings. Those parents would give anything for a room cluttered with a pile of stuff and an eager little one there to help sort through the pieces, and here I was grumbling.

It is so easy to lose perspective.

Sadly, it's often when we lose the things that matter that we regain the perspective of how much those things, those people, matter to us. It baffles my mind how quickly I lose sight of the joy in the gifts of life right in front of my face.

But how do we keep perspective?

Choose something, a daily task—laundry, dishes, folding clothes, picking up—and make it a benchmark, a reminder, for you to remember the preciousness of the life in front of you. And make the benchmark something that is the most unglamorous, like vacuuming. I've found that when you lose normal, you miss those things the most and long for the days when you can simply vacuum a room with your seven-year-old sitting on the bed cleaning beside you.

Life is good.

Life is a gift.

Life is precious.

Don't let the mundane moments in life rob you of the beauty of normal that surrounds you.

Remind yourself to look for the beauty, the gems tucked within the fabric of the everyday normal. Force yourself to see and be thankful for those blessings.

Don't lose sight of the good.

Vacuuming is beautiful.

It's a representation of normal, and normal, my dear friends, is an absolute gift.

Celebrate normal.

Keep perspective. Savor today. Love the little things.

fifteen

---

one mile

Perspective is humbling.

Several years ago, reports of a tornado in Oklahoma flooded my news stream. The tornado had taken lives and caused devastation. Yet that very night after watching live coverage, I tucked my sweet little boy Samuel into his bed and still replied "not now" to reading him a bedtime story.

Many times he asked me to read him just one book. And several times I told him no. I wish I could figure out a reason, but really, it was just because I had things to do. And then, as I pulled the room-darkening shades and picked up the matchbox cars, I remembered the tornado and knew that these moments with a three-year-old asking for his momma to read him a book are actually gifts tucked into the fabric of time. It was as if the flood of perspective rushed over me: those who lost children in that tornado are missing these moments entirely.

Soon after that Oklahoma tornado, my kids were playing outside with neighbor friends just after a wicked storm had passed. As they ran in the sun, it started to hail. Now I realize, in hindsight, that hail falling in bright sun with black clouds all around should have been a clue that severe weather hadn't left. And then as I scanned the sky over my neighbor's home, I saw a funnel cloud forming and dropping down. Despite the kids shouting that it was sunny and great outside, I yelled for all of them to get in their homes as quickly as possible. Within seconds of my kids rushing down the stairs to the corner of the basement, the sirens began to sound. It was a tiny tornado—an F1— that cut a path through the farms to the west of us and destroyed a house about a mile away.

Perspective: the width of the tornado that had devastated Oklahoma was the distance from my house to my neighbor's house that was damaged this time.

That humbles me greatly. I look at my neighborhood—with its manicured yards, petunias hanging from porches, Little Tike toys in the backyard, budding trees—and I think about how I so quickly lost perspective and gratitude. Those harsh wake-up calls about horrible things happening in the world instantly put the important things back into perspective. Then those moments in the bedroom with my three-year-old suddenly become more poignant, more important, and something to embrace.

Yes, Samuel, let's read a story.

I rested on a pillow next to him, reading books about winter with animals gathering sticks and coal to build a snowman, and then about spring with its glorious sounds and sights, and he sighed contently as the words left my mouth. It was normal, that beautiful normal, tucked into a world with so much devastation. You and I and the next person have this challenge, this battle cry: to keep our perspective on "normal" and its beauty. We need to embrace living a life that at its core has a profound gratitude for the simple, often forgotten, moments.

One mile wide.

Drive a mile today. Walk a mile. Get perspective on a mile.

Then, when you walk back into your life and into your mothering journey, bring that frame of mind with you. Slow down just for a bit, hug your children, tell them you love them, call a few friends and thank them or being in your life, say no to the less urgent matters and yes to your kids.

Read the book.

Hold them longer in the rocking chair.

Appreciate the normal beauty in your life.

Gratitude changes perspective.

sixteen

---

little boy with celiac disease

(This letter was written specifically to myself, as a mother whose little one has Celiac Disease—an autoimmune disease where someone can never eat gluten again. Yet I believe that its truths are applicable to many other times when life isn't perfect and we're forced to create a new normal. In fact, one of my beliefs is that when we can allow ourselves to feel and grieve the not-so-fair moments in life, then we are creating space for healing in the future. I hope this letter will speak to mothers who are healing from the not-so-fair moments in their mom journey.)

I know you cried in the grocery store.

It was in the baking aisle, by the flour, with the big sale signs hanging on the shelves. You were standing there looking at the flour and then in your own cart. At the 16-ounce bag of almond flour that will cost you $12 and the sweet rice flour. Then you saw the shelves loaded with heavy bags of white unbleached wheat flour.

And you started to cry.

Not a big sob, but the kind of cry that can't be helped. It's the cry that comes deep from within. Those tears of sadness filled your eyes as you glanced at the lady next to you freely loading her cart with five-pound bags of flour.

Gluten.

Did you ever think that last year was the last year—the last time baking with wheat flour? Did you appreciate that baking? More than likely, you didn't realize what a gift it was not having to think about food and gluten every single day. Did you even really know what gluten was? Or that you would hunt it out to make sure it never entered your Samuel's little body?

You're tired.

You're a fighter.

But you need to cry.

Everyone knows you are strong, that you'll do anything for your boy, and that you want to find joy. But sometimes, especially right now, as you near the anniversary of his diagnosis, you need to mourn. Don't start rationalizing that it's not that bad or it could be worse or we'll just get through.

You'll never be able to put that white unbleached flour on sale for $2.49 in your cart.

That's why you cried. Not because you are selfish or thinking only of yourself. You cried because you love your boy. Fiercely.

Crying doesn't make you weak or make you not appreciate where you are or that you're not grateful.

Crying makes you real.

You didn't choose Celiac Disease for Samuel. You wanted him to be able to eat the Christmas cookies with the wheat flour. To be what you used to think was normal. Sometimes you mourn, and that's OK. But I've seen you fight as well. There's a tension in life, a balance, and living in that place can bring joy.

Don't hide.

Crying and mourning aren't signs of weakness. They are clues that a mother is a fighter, an advocate, a real mom with real emotions who loves her child fiercely. Don't hide from them. Embrace them, use them.

Samuel is worth those fighting tears.

You'll make new traditions, new cookies, and you will find joy.

You hear me? Normal will return.

Normal—that crazy thing that we don't realize how much we love until it's taken from us—will come back. It might not be the same normal, but it will be a new, wonderful normal.

Cookies will be made.

Life will move forward.

And you will, once again, find joy.

the big deal

*I once thought that motherhood
was about the big deals.
But then, as the years ticked by,
I started to realize that
most of motherhood is learning
to celebrate and recognize
the power of the small things.
Simple, no one sees, moments.
A hug in the middle of the night, noses wiped,
carpool waiting lines, frozen dinners, walks,
homework, laundry folded, prayers prayed.
And in the end those small deals add up to
the most magnificent big deal:
your story.*

—Rachel Marie Martin
Findingjoy.net

section five

———

crazy days of motherhood

seventeen

_____

mom. mom. mom.

"Mom, I have a question."

"Mom, can I have a snack?"

"Mom, can you help?"

"Mom, I need you."

"Mom, mom, mom."

Sometimes I wonder how many times in a single day the name "mom" is said to me. I wonder how many times in a month, a year, a decade.

Ten thousand? One hundred thousand? Some days it feels like it's hundreds of times in a day.

"Mom. Mom. Mom."

Sometimes it's the sweetest sound. It makes my heart burst. Sometimes it's annoying—especially when it's the long drawn out "Moooommm!" when there's a fight.

Sometimes I can tell instantly they need me. Sometimes I can tell instantly they want something.

Sometimes it brings good news behind. Sometimes it brings discussion and tears.

Sometimes the words "I hate you" come before. Sometimes the words "I'm sorry" follow.

"Mom."

Who would have imagined so many, many, many meanings?

Sometimes late at night, when the house is finally quiet, the overwhelming beauty of being their person, their mom, hits my heart.

I'm their rock.

I'm their rules.

I'm their safe place.

I'm their constant.

I'm their test the boundaries.

I'm their sit next to them while they do homework.

I'm their cheerleader.

I'm their driver.

I'm their middle-of-the-night person.

I'm their advocate.

I'm their person.

Their mom.

Sweet sister don't ever think all you do doesn't make a difference. Don't doubt your importance. Don't ever go there.

Instead, listen, believe me—you are amazing.

You are their mom.

today

Love others
for who they are.
See the beauty in
the journey.
Hold your head high
and be brave.
Extend a hand, give back.
and believe in the
power of simply
being kind.

—Rachel Marie Martin
Findingjoy.net

eighteen

---

don't lose your happy

The other day a friend of mine told me to have fun with my kids.

I replied, "I don't know if I know how to do that anymore."

Just typing that brings tears to my eyes.

I know how to be the busy mom—moving from one urgent matter to another: *there's no toilet paper, the toilet's overflowing, the kids are fighting, the smoke detector is going off, and I can't find my kid's math sheet that was due three days ago.*

I've mastered the art of hectic mornings—building lunches with almost bare pantries and finding last-minute presents and helping with homework that should have been done the night before but now it is 7:11 a.m. and we need to leave at 7:18 a.m. kind of mornings.

I've figured out how to survive on three hours of interrupted, feet-in-my-face, kids-waking-up sleep. I know the quickest way to Starbucks and that on certain days, like today, it is perfectly acceptable to order the extra shot of espresso and to get it extra hot and maybe with a bit more sugar. I determined that making my bed isn't required, but the kitchen island better stay clean or it's a green light telling everyone that the rest of the house is OK to be messed up.

I've mastered counting to ten many times in a row, gathering my resolve, and dealing with stress. I listen to music to calm me down or I try to take an extra-long shower so I can have four minutes of quiet.

But having fun? Laughing? Just being the happy mom?

Sometimes I fear I've lost it in the busy and the stress.

I'll try to play a game with my kids, but while they're drawing cards and laughing, I'll be creating a new list of things I've forgotten to do and need to do and don't really want to do but can't put off much longer. I might even be thinking about hiding the card that brings you back to the beginning of Candyland, because that game is never-ending. Yeah, that's a skill of motherhood: perfecting the art of not going back to the Candy Cane Forest.

Please don't get me wrong, I love my kids.

But sometimes I feel guilt. Guilt about not being more present or laughing more or having fun or not doing all the cool things that I think my kids deserve. I'll feel guilt about having to work and telling them to give me fifteen more minutes to get this done and then those fifteen minutes turn to thirty and then they're on to something else. It's mom pressure that I don't think we talk about.

I want to be the happy-go-lucky mom. But being a mom is hard.

I'm not complaining. I'm just talking about some of those truths that moms deal with. Like Saturday: I spent almost an hour going back and forth with a very crabby five-year-old who refused to get dressed. Sounds simple, right? Like there's a five-step program to fixing this? Well, in that moment, there wasn't. I felt like I wasn't a good mom because we were battling over putting on clean underwear and pants and a shirt.

Where did the happy part go?

The truth is: we need to acknowledge that some seasons in our life are just hard work. Motherhood being one of them. But just because it's hard or we lost that happy for a bit doesn't make us a bad mom.

Still, I want happy to return. So I'm deciding to do one thing every day that makes me happy. One thing. Maybe it's listening to music that I love or spending thirty minutes watching *Modern Family* on Hulu. Maybe it's cleaning up my Facebook stream and getting rid of people who cause me angst. Maybe it's deciding to play that game with my kids but giving myself grace if I start thinking about the dishes that need to be done as I flip over the double yellow card.

And let me offer that to you too: Do one thing that makes you happy.

It's about grace today. And knowing that happy can come back.

Allow yourself a moment when the cares of the world and the never-ending to-dos can fall off your back. Take a deep breath and fill your head with words about the awesome that you do, versus all the things you didn't do.

You're doing unbelievable things. Even if it feels ordinary and exasperating and tiring.

With love. Hope. And the words "I'm proud of you" to all of you today.

Happy can be there.

We didn't forget.

We just got busy.

nineteen

_____

overwhelmed

Today that was me.

I walked into my messy home with its sick children, laundry to do, groceries to buy, dishes to wash, lawn to be mowed, and a to-do list longer than one side of paper.

When your to-do list needs to be categorized, you know you're in too deep.

I wanted to sit in the corner, put my head in my lap, and have a good cry.

But then there was my two-year-old saying my name, the four-year-old jumping on the stairs, my six-year-old asking to play a game of Slap Jack, my sick eight-year-old having a coughing fit, my 10-year-old refusing to unload the dishes, my 14-year-old who was supposed to teach ballet (yes, she teaches ballet), and my almost 16-year-old who needed to rest because she was also getting sick.

And I needed to make dinner but, between you and me, I could not find my kitchen counter.

Being overwhelmed isn't what motherhood and life is about, and yet it happens. Or maybe feeling this way is a part of life and instead of wondering, _how in the world did I get here again?_ we just need to look straight at it and remind ourselves of a bit of truth. So here's what I remembered, looking at every single thing on that way too long list on that crazy day in my life: It won't last. This is a temporary situation, and this too shall pass.

Overwhelm, as hard and horrible as it is in that moment, simply will not last forever.

If you feel overwhelmed, you are not alone. But we don't talk about overwhelm, because we think we're the only ones who want to lock ourselves in the bathroom and have a good cry. We just start to compare and think that being a good mom means never getting to this place. So let me remind you: you are not the only mom who feels overwhelmed.

Life pushes so much on our plate. It's exhausting and can feel very lonely. But all those to-dos don't define us as mothers.

Do not measure your worth based on what you have left to do.

So, awesome, tired, and feeling overwhelmed mom: you *will* move out of this feeling. I know you will. I did. My counters were still buried, my dishes waiting to be done and the house a mess. Yet I found a change of my heart and perspective.

At first, I saw too much to do and wanted everything done immediately. Not possible. So instead, I prayed, drank some coffee, and made a choice to change my perspective. Then I did one thing: I sat down, watched two little boys of mine blowing bubbles into their iced tea, and laughed. I found a bit of joy that I had been missing once I let overwhelm go. It's not dependent upon having everything perfect.

You're stronger than overwhelm too. If you need help, don't be afraid to ask for it. It takes a village!

So mothers, stand up, brush yourself off, and find one thing to do. Hug those kids. Play with them. Let them make you laugh.

You will beat overwhelm. It is the thief of joy.

keep trying

Listen, the quote,
"fall seven times, stand up eight"
doesn't tell you to never fall.
You know why?
You WILL fall in life.
That's okay.
What really matters
is that you are brave enough
to stand up and try again.
Keep standing up.
Change never happens sitting still.

—Rachel Marie Martin
Findingjoy.net

twenty

---

keep trying

I've been a mom for over twenty years. People think that such a magical double decade number means I've discovered the secret of being a good mom. Or a creative mom. Or the cool mom. Or a patient mom. They even ask me.

It's pretty much at that asking moment when I will lose my patience in Starbucks or Target or Kroger, so they change the request from patience or creativity and simply wonder about the secret to being a *successful, good-kids-turn-out-OK-and-I'm happy* mom. (They can see that patience might not be mastered.)

When they ask, I laugh. Or chuckle. Or get teary. Because truthfully, there is no secret.

I know because I searched for it for so many of my mom years. I looked and hoped and always felt like I fell just a bit short. I hate that feeling. Don't you? That feeling like everyone else has it together and *if I'm just a little bit better* then maybe I, too, can figure this whole mom thing out and win.

Because, to be honest, for so much of my motherhood journey I've felt like I've been failing. I've cried so many times, wondered why it was hard, and hoped and prayed that maybe just one day I'd cross that finish line successfully.

But as we all learn, there isn't a handbook of forty-two ways to make a dinner that everyone will love. There's no way to defeat the crazy teenager rebellion years with a smile and a latte. What works for bedtime for one kid *will not work* for the next. Potty training is just always torture, no matter what anyone says. Don't listen to them.

Middle school is where I lost my patience. I felt a reprieve when they were seven, eight, and nine, but then as soon as I thought, *I've figured it out!* they got to preteen stuff. Humbling. It's like a giant do-over moment.

Sitting in a car when they are learning to drive is terrifying, pure and simple. It's like payback in a way, as if God is laughing at us because we muttered, *Won't it be nice when they grow up and drive themselves places?*

But through all of my motherhood journey, at each age and stage, I have simply wanted to be a good mom. And I've learned that it takes a lot of trying.

So much trying that I mutter the quote "fall seven times, stand up eight" during many a morning rush or at bedtime or during homework. To be fully transparent, there are nights when I go to bed ticked off at my kids. Other nights where I go to bed ticked off at myself because I felt I *should have could have* done something different. There are some days I wish would last forever and some days I wish would be over when it's only seven a.m.

It's really not about doing anything better. Trust me. **It's about showing up every single day.** It's about figuring out dinner when the pantry is empty and every single person in your house says they are absolutely starving. It's about showing up for events when your ex is there and you are uncomfortable and you don't know what to do but smile and cheer. It's about walking into doctor's offices and principal's offices.

Showing up means emailing teachers to talk about grades and sitting up helping with projects that cost you thirty dollars and seem pointless but need to get done.

You want the best *good mom* secret? It's what you're already doing every single day: trying.

When you stop, when you throw in the towel, those are the moments when you quit. And quitting? That's the one thing you don't do. You know why I know?

You're here. Right now, reading these words, wanting to know the secret. Why would you even care about the secret if you didn't care? But you do care. You love those kids who make you feel you're the worst mom in the world at times. You love those kids you give up sleep for. You love them even when they drive you absolutely crazy. Oh, sweet mom, listen: even if you are *tired worn out overwhelmed exhausted worried fearful joyful content,* you need to know one thing: you are the good mom secret.

You are the one your kids love even if they say they hate you.

You are the one who makes your house their home.

You are the one they search for in the crowd and smile at.

You are the one they need when they are sick or afraid or need to come home.

You are the one who matters to the people who matter the most.

Your family.

So carry on. Don't waste time worrying that you're not enough. Don't chase for the secret. Just keep showing up, trying, loving, giving, hoping. Day after day, night after night.

That's the good mom secret.

a real mom

Emotional, yet the rock.
Tired, but keeps going.
Worried, but full of hope.
Impatient, yet patient.
Overwhelmed, but never quits.
Amazing, even though doubted.
Wonderful, even in the chaos.
Life changer, every single day.

—Rachel Marie Martin
Findingjoy.net

section six

―――――――

motherhood is not for wimps

twenty-one

---

the hard days

To the out-of-breath mom who wants to throw in the towel on a hard day: if you pick the towel back up soon after it hits the floor, you are going to be OK. And even if you choose to leave it on the floor, you will still be OK.

Let's face it, we are talking about the hard days. Because they happen. So now it's about what we need to do on those days. I am talking about the day that goes off track first thing in the morning and you want to throw your arms in the air and grab the Ben and Jerry's from the freezer. Turn on Netflix and binge-watch a marathon of feel-good movies. Do something just for you.

Just take a breath and stop for a moment. Just for a minute and listen.

I know it's hard. I know about the spills, the relationships, the laundry that smells because it was left in the washer too long, the peanut butter smashed on the floor. There is literally nothing for breakfast and there's no coffee—just an empty Keurig box that taunts you. The kids are fighting, toys are dumped, books torn, the yard is full toys. You're starting to wonder if the weather is making all the kids crabby at the same time, and all of yesterday's dishes are sitting on the table, and you'd just like a shower, and you're late, and, and, and. ...

Well, that makes it really hard to find courage and patience and that pull-up-your-bootstraps energy when you're out of breath on a day that all of a sudden feels hard. And that is just the morning.

In fact, often, it feels impossible.

We sit in this place of wondering if it really matters what we do. We're doing it day in and day out and we're still behind and racing to try to catch up to this constantly moving bar of normal. Remember back before the kids were born? And how we dreamed about crafts on the table—we never imagined the spilled glue and glitter and paint on the face. And we never imagined that they wouldn't really care about doing that fabulous fall pumpkin craft. We dreamed of the perfect day with nutritious and organic breakfasts in the Anthropologie-inspired family room with cute baskets and chalk write-on labels and the mornings with a quick check-off routine with laminated charts and adorable stickers.

I remember.

But that? That was just what I thought motherhood would look like. It's what our society via many different types of media made me think it should look like. There are those rare times that some of those perfect moments may work—but, really, the cute wicker baskets with chalk write-on labels? If I had them, those labels would only stay on for a day. So let's just keep it real.

It's hard to remember what we do accomplish because it's stuffed behind layers of to-dos, don't dos, feeling like we'll never measure up, and feeling behind on top of all of that. That's why I want us to all stop, slow down, and embrace the motherhood journey.

Maybe it's crazy and chaotic and loud and frantic, but also tucked deep within are moments that will be gone one day. The kids will grow, the noise will lessen, the kitchen counters will stay clean, we'll get all the sleep we want, and we'll only have a couple loads of laundry a week. And you know what? We'll miss the crazy, chaotic, throw-in-the-towel kind of days, just a little bit.

I know it's hard to see that while in the trenches of motherhood.

We're in this race together. You and me and the other moms who are reading this collection of letters.

Don't throw in the towel. If you do, take a deep breath, and pick it back up and wipe off some dishes. Because we can't give up. We have to continue fighting the good fight even on the hard days. Oh, and I can't say enough that asking for help is brave. Don't wait and don't feel bad about asking. That's what friends and family are for.

Now, pick yourself up, and let's do this day well. Sending hugs your way.

twenty-two

---

a "yes" mom

I'm just not a "yes" mom. I wrote years and years ago about how I
wanted to be that mom. It became like a notch on the mom ladder that
I was determined to reach. I wanted to be the one who would say, "You
want to make slime? Sure! That would be great! I will clean it all up. No
problem. Don't worry about the mess."

But I'm not. I'm not. I hear about slime, and the hair on my neck
stands up and I want to see if there is wine in the fridge.

I don't think I would have had the bravery to admit to you that silly
little fact, except, well, I know most of you who deal with slime
creators get it. Trust me, I wanted to be the "yes" mom. I wanted to
sprinkle their world with an abundance of yes moments. I try. I really
do, but I cannot live always saying yes. I cannot. My sanity cannot
handle it all the time.

I cannot do Elf on the Shelf. I cannot do the Tooth Fairy every
time. I cannot volunteer all the time. I cannot do random slime
creations. I cannot allow ultimate freedom. I cannot just drop everything. I cannot say "yes" to so much. I just cannot.

And I'm OK with that.

**Because I am a better mom when I give myself the grace to
say no and *breathe*.**

Sometimes I just don't want my kitchen looking like a lab experiment. I know it provides creativity, connection, and so forth, but sometimes, I just like to see my counters. And I like having limits. I don't care that my kids tell me that "my friend's parents let them have this app" because, well, these are my kids and I have decided that there is no way that app or game is coming in my house. I'm OK that I have never done Elf on the Shelf. I think all the parents who do are cool, but I have gotten to the point where I'm OK that we don't.

I'm OK with the power of yes and no. I think the social media-driven world we live in makes us think, whether we realize it or not, that we have to *do everything* we see that everyone else does.

You just don't.

You don't have to do all those things. You don't. All that social media? It's the yes moment highlight reel of all our lives.

That part is awesome. However, and pay attention: it is not the to-do list for each of us. There is a difference between observing and cheering each other on and thinking we have to do everything that everyone else is doing and then deciding that doing all of that makes us a better mom. We all get to pick and choose our yes moments. That's so easy to forget when we scroll down on our phones and see what everyone else is doing.

So I quit being the yes mom to the world's list and became a yes mom for my family's list.

Mothering is enough without feeling the constant pressure of everyone else's yes.

That was in all caps and bold so you can read it twice. Or pretend I am yelling it to you across the table at Starbucks.

You know what you need to say yes to? Yourself. Your heart.

Don't say yes because of guilt or expectations. The most powerful thing you can do is create your own moments of crazy *yes* and crazy *no way*. And you know what this gives you? Margin. Space. Time to mother. Time to love. Time to make slime (haha). Time to give.

Time to be. Breathing room.

Let's say yes to that.

It's OK, my friend, to not do everything. In fact, I can guarantee you right now that saying no will be the most wonderful gift you can give your kids. You know why? Because you are mothering them. Not doing what is hypothetically expected. You are instead, being you, loving your family, and mothering.

Say yes to that and the rest will fall into place.

twenty-three

_____

the mom I said I would never be

I don't know how it happened, honestly. But it totally, one hundred percent, happened.

Let's cut to the chase. First, there are fruit snacks in my cupboard, and they aren't organic, and even if they were, *organic fruit snacks* sound like an oxymoron to me. Yet I love those colorfully packaged faux healthy snacks because the kids ask me, "Can I have a snack" and I can say, "Yeah, sure, grab a fruit snack!" and they cheer, and I emphasize the word *fruit* loudly so anyone walking by hears *fruit* and not the snack part. Silly, right?

When I became a mom (over twenty years ago, but who's counting), I was the mom who vowed to never purchase one ounce of junk food ever. And that my vehicle would never be a minivan (even though I am loving mine right now). My firstborn daughter was growing so fast, and I had another daughter and another and, well, you get the story. I now sport my minivan everywhere and my life has changed. We even go through the drive-through at Starbucks so often that the employees recognize my voice and know that my new favorite drink is a grande two pump caramel latte.

I was positive that I was not going to lose my cool, ever. Nope. I was going to be the ultimate baby-whispering mom, that is until real motherhood hit. Whispering was driving me crazy and making me lose my voice, but it transformed into a raspy yell. So now I try to not yell, but sometimes I do, like the other night when my twelve-year-old was out biking and his phone died, it was after dark and I couldn't find him. So when I found him by the community pool at the park, I did *not* whisper out of my very cool black minivan but rather yelled loudly, so all his friends could hear: "You are grounded!"

I made sure it was extra loud. I was super mad but also super scared, and I thought that his friends all needed to hear what happens when you don't come home when your parents expect you.

But, you know, I never thought I was going to do that.

I never considered that my kids would have free will. The free will variable of motherhood that Hallmark and friends with no kids forget to tell you about.

And as a result, I've learned that I am the mom I said I never would be. I'm way cooler now. I know exactly what really matters. The fruit snacks. They don't define me as a mom. Nor does having all organic foods in my cabinet. None of the things that I thought were critical have any ounce of mom value.

Instead, it's about balance, about grace, and learning to figure out what works for our families.

Maybe we Facebook all our kids' moments. Maybe we love to decorate everything and have the perfect birthday parties—the ones I can't muster up.

Maybe we work, maybe we stay at home. Maybe we have tons of kids, maybe one.

Maybe we breastfed, maybe we formula fed. Maybe we love fruit snacks, maybe we think they're evil.

Maybe we vowed "no electronics," maybe we love electronics.

Maybe we are not the mom we said we would ever be.

It's all OK, and it's cool to do what works for you and your family.

Do you know why I *love* that I am not the mom I said I would be?

It's because I realized life was too short to stick to an idea that didn't work.

I let my babies sleep with me. We don't eat gluten (because my son has Celiac Disease). My kids, at least the little ones, eat hot lunch at school. My vehicle is a minivan, and it's awesome. I run in the morning. I work. Sometimes I have a glass of wine. I lose my patience too often. I curse at laundry. I tell the kids, "Don't you love me? Why is this so hard?" and then in the next breath I tell them, "I will love you always." I'v been a single mom. I once was married. My kitchen has stuff on the counter. My kids have phones. They love Netflix too. My kids know they are not to eat on the couch but today I steam cleaned out stains from Doritos. Yeah, I buy them too.

Life is OK without having all the answers or being perfect.

It really is. Way too many of my friends have endured the death of a child. And not *one* of them was like, "Thank God I followed all the rules I had for myself and pushed myself to be perfect." Nope.

We all want time. Grace. Margin. And space to laugh.

So with that, I tell you: I am so far from the mom I said I would be.

And I love myself.

And I love our story.

twenty-four

---

you're not the only one

Who thinks she's the only mom who doesn't have it all together?

Or worries about her kids.

Or thinks that she's not doing good enough.

You're not the only one who wakes up each morning determined to make it a great day, only to sometimes fall flat on her face with frustration by 6:49 a.m. when her kindergartner decides he doesn't like any of the shirts she's given him and her third grader forgot to do his homework and the van won't start.

Or signs that reading list and decides to include the reading on Minecraft as part of the required twenty minutes of reading. Or gets so tired of trying to figure out what to put in those lunch boxes day after day after day and somedays just kind of begs the kids to take hot lunch. Just once.

You're not the only mom wondering how the house got so messy when she just cleaned it and why on earth everyone stops over during those times and not when it's immaculate.

Or wishes there were extra money in the checking account to just order dinner in.

You're not the only mom who deals with guilt for the littlest things.

Or laughs at the sweetest things her kids say—even when she's the only one who gets it.

You're not the only mom in the school pickup line who wonders why no one is moving forward.

Or wonders why all the other parents seem to have it all together while she just changed from yoga pants to jeans ten minutes prior to leaving. Or hopes for no homework because she's just a bit tired of drilling state abbreviations. Again.

You're not the only mom who wonders if what she's doing makes a difference.

Or wishes for a break but won't admit that because no one else ever says that out loud.

You're not the only mom who reads articles on Facebook and then feels so alone.

Or scours pins on Pinterest looking for the fails, so there's a bit of hope.

You're not the only mom who's told to embrace every moment but sometimes has the hardest time remembering that.

Or gets frustrated when the kids won't go to bed and wonders *why on earth is this so hard?*

You're not the only mom who thinks that her boys have no aim and wishes she had stock in Lysol.

Or reruns the wash because she forgot about it last night. Or has a massive basket of unmatched socks that one day she just decides to throw out, and then the next day finds one of the missing socks tucked under the foot of a kid's bed along with half a dozen wrappers and orange peels.

You're not the only mom who looks in the mirror and is surprised at the reflection and wonders when those wrinkles showed up in the corner of her eyes and if there's a miracle cream to make them vanish just a bit.

Or wonders why embracing aging isn't that simple.

You're not the only mom who is super grateful for Netflix or Hulu or YouTube or those tablets, because they give her a break.

Or worries that she's letting her kids use too much media. Or wishes she actually enjoyed playing some of those kid games. But let's face it, there is only so many times you can slide on Chutes and Ladders before it's enough.

You're not the only mom who counts pennies or tries to stretch a dollar.

Or puts out the presents on the bed and tries to make sure they're equal. Or gives up stuff for herself so that the kids can have more.

You're not the only mom who doesn't have the perfect Hallmark life.

Or is single and wishing for some peace in the midst of crazy and sometimes just feels sad. Or has support and love and is so thankful.

You're not the only mom who sometimes feels alone. Because let's face it, sometimes it's so easy to feel alone in this massive journey called motherhood. Especially when we feel like we're the only mom in the world who has....

Well, as you can see, you're probably not the only mom.

In fact, there are so many of us. Tripping, falling, standing up, brushing off, trying again.

You're not the only one. There are many of us walking with you.

Sometimes it just takes a reminder.

truth

Be you.
Be unapologetically yourself.
Follow your dreams.
Fight for your family.
Invest in relationships.
Take care of your body.
Laugh a whole bunch more.
Let yourself feel.
Don't be so hard on yourself.
Push yourself to be better.
Don't settle.
Don't quit on your heart.
Love deeply.
Forgive. Let go.
Tap into your creativity.
Live your life with enthusiasm.

—Rachel Marie Martin
Findingjoy.net

section seven

———

mom truth

twenty-five

it can't be measured

There is no measuring stick.

There isn't a World's Best Mom award out there. There isn't a Pinterest-perfect mom who finishes every single pin on her boards. There isn't a medal for being the skinniest, craftiest, or funniest. There isn't this utopian ideal mom award for the mom who is always clever, witty, and well-dressed in fashionable layers of clothing with the perfect jeans and stylish boots.

The only world's "best mom award" goes to you.

You see, you are absolutely the world's best mom for your family today. Even though sometimes you mess up or don't believe that it's true.

It's easy to think that you don't measure up. I know. Because when I share my heart with you, I'm sharing struggles that I have as well. Sometimes I will go to bed at night and look at my day and think that I messed up again. I'll see the bikes around the yard, the craft projects untouched, and an art board with snowflakes on it even though it's the middle of June. Then I'll remember every place that I think I failed.

But there really isn't failing when you're trying. Instead of sitting in those preconceived failures, think about the good parts of the day.

A hypothetical measuring-up looms over us as moms. We really don't ever seem to get a break. We're being shouted at that we need to do this, make that, wear this, and have everything in order.

It's exhausting. And it often leads to this idea of motherhood that makes us want to put our head in our hands and scream, "I give up! I'll never measure up."

One day we're supposed to be doing this, and the very next morning I read that we shouldn't have done that. Don't use those bottles. Use these. Don't drive this way. Wear these clothes. Teach your child to read by age two. Don't vaccinate. Do vaccinate. Keep a stunning and well-organized Pinterest board. Only cook organic. Shop two times a month. Do once-a-month cooking. Wash your clothes with homemade soap. Make your own living room curtains. Have someone help you clean your house. Get this car seat. Never get fast food. Make homemade Play-Doh. Do this. Do that.

Enough! You know what I want to tell you? Don't think about measuring up. Think about being the best mom you can be right now for your family. Give yourself grace in the morning. Learn from the past. Don't label yourself. Do one thing and do it well. Do your version of "momming."

Just keep trying.

You know what you need to do? **Love your kids. Do your best. Apologize for mistakes. Learn from others. Constantly strive to be better. But in that, understand that you are real.**

Moms, the more real we are with each other, the healthier we can become. Let's be real. Let's help each other. Let's be there for each other. Let's stop trying to impress each other with the facade of having everything perfect, and instead let's be there as friends. Loving on each other when we have a hard day. Cheering for each other for a good day. Not comparing, but rather celebrating each other.

We need more real.

Think about this before you think about measuring up: moms are amazing in their own way.

You are amazing.

You cook, clean, pray, vacuum, fold, wash, help with homework, make meals, sing songs, teach prayers, let your littles grow so they are ready when it's time to leave the nest, wonder, worry, diagnose, lose sleep, get up at dawn, and go to bed after the sun has set. This is amazing.

Brush yourself off, put the measuring stick away, and continue to be amazing.

Because that is exactly what you already are.

twenty-six

how you became a mom

We are all moms.

How we became moms doesn't define our motherhood.

Some of us adopted, fostered, delivered babies with meds or without, had C-sections, IVF—and yet that doesn't matter. We are all still moms at our very core.

But sometimes we struggle.

We may struggle thinking we wish we could have done it differently. We read articles about birth stories or adoption, and then we feel lost wishing that we had a story. Yet, sweet mom, it's truly not about how we became moms that really matters—it is what we do *after* that ultimately matters.

I will repeat it: it's the after that matters most. After I had my son Caleb, I felt defeated. His labor was long and hard, and the medical team had to intervene—things I never wanted to deal with—and then I came home with guilt. Like I wasn't strong enough, worthy enough, brave enough, *if only I had just tried more*. Those days spent home with my sweet boy were being tainted by this idea of how he should have entered my arms. Until one day a friend told me that how he came to me doesn't matter—it's him, in my arms, that matters more than the story of how he got there.

Moms. Listen to me. Please.

I know some of you are hurting right now because you are struggling with your own mom story. You're holding onto labels, hurts, unrealistic expectations, and you are letting them taint the gift of this moment. You see other people's stories and wonder why that wasn't your story, your motherhood journey. It's the end result that matters. Your mom story is personal to you; it makes you a mother.

Sweet mother. Let it go. What matters is today.

Being a mom matters more than how we became moms.

Sweet mom, embrace the child and the gift of being a mother. When they look at you, they see Mom. They will never judge how they came into your life.

Give of yourself. Pray for them. Embrace the ups and downs.

But, ultimately, love them. Unconditionally. Motherhood is a beautiful blessing.

journey

She was on a journey.
It didnt look like the journey
she had planned.
In fact. Sometimes
she felt lost.
That part was hard.
And yet she kept trying.
She kept putting one foot
in front of the other.
She kept moving.
she kept having faith
in the future.
She didn't stop
She kept going.

—Rachel Marie Martin
Findingjoy.net

twenty-seven

---

mom confession

I am writing this in my hallway at the top of the stairs because my two little boys won't stay in their room and go to bed unless I sit up here at the doorway and utter words like "go to bed" and "stay in bed now—I mean it" and "no more water" and "you will lose media time if you get out of your bed again" until they both decide to give in, slip under their covers, and go to sleep.

I've tried charts. Bedtime routines. Stickers. Time outs. All of it. And I've resorted to working at the top of the stairs for an hour each night and muttering those phrases. I've gotten quite used to emailing, Tweeting, Facebooking, and writing with my back against the door to my room and my eyes looking in their room to see if they're asleep.

My life isn't all together. I've got my share—well, more than my share—of ups and downs, fails and do-overs, highs and lows, and sitting at the top of the stairs moments because I can't seem to think of something better to do.

I make boxed macaroni and cheese for lunch with the little powdered cheese. We don't eat organic apples. I buy my kids Fruit Roll-Ups.

Sometimes my kids play too much media.

I skip words—OK, I skip paragraphs—in long books at bedtime.

I don't fold all the little boys' clothes because they dump them out anyway. My sock basket is rarely folded. I don't like doing dishes.

My living room has throw pillows on the floor, papers on the couch, a lamp shade that's crooked, shoes scattered by the door, and a couple empty boxes waiting for the toys to be put away.

My Pinterest board has pictures of perfectly organized rooms.

I love Starbucks and will drive there sometimes with the kids in the back, and then I will take the long way home.

I get impatient with my kids. And I'm normal.

And the kids? Well, they're normal (most of the time). Or as normal as kids who thinks that everything has to be fair are ever going to be.

Motherhood isn't based on perfection. It's not based on being gluten free (which we must have in my world) or whole wheat macaroni with organic apples.

Motherhood is just real.

Real life with real moms who lose their patience, who want to throw in the towel, who have kids (like my Samuel who is in the hallway next to me telling me he doesn't want to go to bed) who don't stay in bed. It's full of moms who have to work who'd rather stay home. Or moms who stay home who'd rather work. Or moms who are simply tired with the everyday same routine.

It's full of real moms who take their kids to the apple orchard and the zoo and the coffee shop and the grocery store and the doctor and school and all that normal stuff. It's full of moms who feel like all they do is the laundry again and again and if they see clean clothes stuffed in the hamper one more time, they threaten to take them away and sell them (or maybe that's just me). It's full of moms who are happy, joyful, sad, overwhelmed, and—let's face it—real.

That's the *being enough* mom. That is mom enough. That's

my confession.

It's not that I don't want to be better. At heart, I think we wake up each day and want to be better than the last. That's why I celebrate pulling up the bootstraps and trying again and giving yourself grace. Motherhood has moments of extreme patience, extreme trying, and really learning not to compare.

Motherhood isn't based on external markers of perfection. Motherhood is an act of learning.

Every single day.

It's being OK with the fact that you like the convenience of boxed macaroni and cheese. You know why? Because your contentment is not based on what other moms are doing—it's based on you—on you knowing your family, knowing what is best for your family, and being brave and confident in what you're doing.

Motherhood, and in fact, life, is often this journey of waking up and discovering self.

You the mother, in whatever stage of motherhood you may find yourself, are doing just fine. You are doing fine even if your kids don't stay in bed, you hate potty training (does anyone like that one?), your kids have meltdowns in the store, you get exasperated, and you sneak the last spoonful of ice cream for yourself. Just keep trying, keep doing your best, and keep growing more confident in your ability to mother.

You know what your kids need? Of course, you do. They don't need perfect. They need you.

You, the wonderfully imperfect mom.

That's my mom confession today.

Oh yes, and we're having hot dogs and peaches and macaroni and cheese for lunch tomorrow.

twenty-eight

take a break

I run on empty.

I tell myself it's not really empty and *it's just what moms do* and I try to not look at that blinking gauge that's signaling that it's almost empty, and yet I push and push.

I think it's noble. The push. The forgetting of self. It's the nature of our society to push everything until the last drop.

We wait to get gas till the light warns us that the tank is empty; we save the last drops of milk; we scrape the peanut butter from the sides of the jar—and we do the same with our self. We push and give and often ignore the warning lights telling us to refuel.

It's hard to remember that *you matter* when you're exhausted.

In fact, when we're exhausted it's so ridiculously hard to keep perspective because we're just trying to get the next thing done on the list of never-ending to-dos. We go into a survival mode.

I look at culture and society from years past. I look at the support that women surrounded themselves with: time together, helping each other, that utopian idea of barn building. We don't seem to have much of that in our culture, especially the community. Instead, we have weeks crammed full—packed with tremendous amounts of things to do and pressures and deadlines, without much space in the hyper schedule to simply chill.

Moms, there is no guilt in needing a break.

I believe that, in order to give, you must make sure that you are replenished. Sometimes we don't talk about that need. We brush it under the table and ignore it with *I'm great* and *no worries*, and yet we're burning out.

If your tank is dangerously low all the time, then you will lose sight of the beautiful extraordinary role that motherhood has in your life and the lives of your children. It can slip into drudgery. And in the trenches will come discontent, sadness, fatigue, and disillusionment.

I know. I've felt it. Oh my goodness yes, I have lost the joy and happiness in life many times just simply trying to survive from one day to the other. I starved myself from my own needs and martyred and felt guilt over saying no to the busy and yes to myself.

So I've learned to take breaks. Yoga here. Coffee time. And then, a couple years ago, by an absolute gift, a week in South Carolina with some sweet girlfriends. We had grand plans—go dolphin watching, visit shops, tour. And yet we spent hours sitting at the edge of the Atlantic with the surf washing over us. We just sat. And talked. And sat. And decompressed.

Moms need moments of still.

Let me repeat that: you need moments of still.

Moments where you can just be you.

I know it's hard. I cried when I left home for those eight days last year. But I came home better, stronger, and more intentional.

This post isn't about hopping on a plane and leaving. Even though there are days when that seems the ideal option. And feeling like that? That's not bad—so no guilt for those feelings either. We're all real here, and in that realness, we're admitting that there are days when we've had enough crazy and need a break.

This is about recognizing the need for rest and recharging that is so easy to overlook.

You see, for years I didn't give myself permission to leave. I'd come up with excuse after excuse not to take care of myself, all in the name of motherhood. And I became worn out.

Recognize that some days it is OK to let the kids watch a movie while you grab your favorite book, a cup of chai, and just read. Maybe you schedule a date with friends to grab coffee. Maybe you go in the backyard and work on your garden. Maybe you stay up late with ice cream to watch a movie. Maybe you take the long way home. Maybe pizza is the answer. Maybe a weekend getaway.

You must take care of yourself.

If you don't, you can burn out. I did. I just didn't realize it because I was so stubborn in thinking that the right way to be a mother was to never stop giving, and I forgot to take care of me.

I'm giving you permission to give yourself a break.

It doesn't make you less of a mother. Not at all. In fact, by cultivating space within your schedule to take care of you, you might become a better, more intentional, mother.

I write. I play piano. I speak. I read. I garden. I travel. I drink coffee at Starbucks. And I have days where I'm super thankful for Hulu or Netflix or Minecraft. And that is all good. Recharge, sweet mother, recharge.

constant

*You are your
children's constant.
You are unconditional love.
You are showing up.
You are not giving up.
You are encouragement.
You are boundaries.
You are courage.
You are their mom.
They don't need perfection.
They just need you.
Their constant.*

—Rachel Marie Martin
Findingjoy.net

section eight

———

for those days with littles

twenty-nine

---

a new baby

(This letter was inspired by the five hours I was blessed to watch my dear friend Maria's two-month-old daughter, Emma. Spending time with her reminded me of those days when I'd have new little ones in my home. It brought back the memories of those days when I was so grateful just to get dinner on the table. Memories.)

Your main goal right now?

To be a mom to that sweet little baby.

I know. You're reading this thinking about all that you have to do.

Or more than that, you're thinking about all that you got done right before the baby came home. Remember those days of nesting? The cleaning and sorting and cleaning again and de-cluttering? Of course, you do. But you can't do that right now. You can't be thinking about those tasks or how behind you are from your pre-baby routine. Let go of the worry that you're behind—it will only frustrate—and instead simply expect that your life won't feel balanced or normal. When you have a new baby in your home, life will feel out of balance.

That's normal.

There is new life, new joys, new laughter, new energy, new smiles—that you, the mom gets blessed to share every day. But, dear moms with little babies, it is also completely exhausting. You are on demand every single second of the day and night. You get little sleep. Your house is in disarray. You can't remember what it's like to be caught up on laundry. You are lucky if dinner is done before seven p.m.

Give. Give. Give.

The days blur into weeks and you're tired. And after a while, you kind of wish for the order that you had in those earlier weeks. Oh, I know you love that little one. I've been blessed to bring home seven little babes. And seven times I've had to relearn how to do life. Yes, that's it. It's a surrender of control and willingness to embrace a new version of normal.

So I'm telling you that if you are offered help, take it. I don't care if the laundry is piled up. If someone wants to help, then you open your door, smile with your tired smile, and let them bless you.

Don't apologize for the piles of laundry or messy floors or your hair. That's OK. You're doing something amazing right now: nurturing a baby full time. You will have your turn to bless others, but right now when you have a new little one in your home, you need to be blessed.

But what if you don't have help?

Then you need to give yourself extra grace. And you, tired blessed mom with your newborn, you choose one thing each day to accomplish. Do it in bits throughout the day, and when you are overwhelmed or tired, look at what you've finished.

Give yourself grace.

Your home, especially in those early newborn months, is not a reflection of who you are and your homemaking skills. This is a new normal. Just when you find your routine, your little one will have a milestone to celebrate that will change everything once again. I remember thinking that I would have to buy diapers forever, but just like that, they were potty-trained. No more diapers. But it is worth it.

Relish these days—these sweet babymoon days. I look back and remember those little babies that were content to sit in my arms. (When they sleep, you simply must rest, and that is good.) I know it's a blur, and it's oh so tiring, but there is something almost magical (even in the exhaustion) about holding teeny, little ones who just need their mom.

They'll grow, and these busy days will just be a distant memory.

Sit now, hold your little one in your arms, and look at that teeny face, that face that will someday call you momma, and rest in the joy and the gift of being a mother.

Rest. Do your one thing. Accept help. Breathe. And don't compare the normal of right now to your future normal. The normal will come and go, and with it will be an integration of a new little one into your life.

You, mom of a little baby, are blessed.

Busy, exhausted, craving normal and sleep, but blessed.

Enjoy your babymoon.

It will soon be a memory.

thirty

---

days with littles

You amaze me.

Yes, I know you might read this and think that I have seven kids and wonder why I am writing a letter to you. But you see, yesterday I was reminded how hard it is to be a mom to the little ones. My older girls were gone—at ballet and with a friend—and my older boys were at Taekwondo. Leaving me home. Alone. With my very busy toddler Samuel and extremely precocious preschooler Elijah.

Oh my goodness.

I've forgotten how busy those years were with just those littles underfoot. There was running, jumping, loud noises, needing me, and lots of busy activity. I needed to get the kitchen cleaned and dinner made, and then the phone rang and, well, it was just me.

You mothers of littles, I know that sometimes your days are a blur and you feel like you don't get much accomplished, but the truth is: you do a ton. You work hard teaching the little ones to be independent.

They don't sit still—you don't sit still. They run around—you run after them. They're hungry (again), you get them food (again). You try to sit down—they pull you up. They dump out the toys—you clean them up. You answer the phone—they start fighting over a toy.

You are busy.

I want you to know that what you are doing in this stage of parenting, even though it just feels so utterly crazy at moments, you will one day look back on and be proud of.

That time, when I had kids under five, was seriously one of the hardest stages in my own parenting journey. Like you, I was needed all day long. It was exhausting. There was no fanfare, no awards, no blue ribbons, nothing.

It's easy to think that what you are doing doesn't matter. That your work—picking up everything, cleaning handprints from the wall, diaper-changing with just one wipe, nose- and cheek-wiping, spoon feeding of yucky smooshed peas, rocking, reading of Dr. Seuss, and more—doesn't matter.

But, dear sister, it matters. Keep loving on your children.

They grow fast, those little ones. And soon the ones dumping out the blocks will be reading, busy on the phone, doing something that doesn't involve you—and you will want them around. You smile while you think back with nostalgia at the days when the little ones were underfoot.

You are amazing.

you matter

*Your day doesn't have
to be perfect
to have meaning.
Showing up matters.
Giving matters.
Trying matters.
Loving matters.
Being there matters.
Perfection doesn't matter.
You matter.*

—Rachel Marie Martin
Findingjoy.net

thirty-one

─────────

little ones crying in the store

Breathe. Just breathe.

We've all been there. In the store, with a little one melting on the floor (the floor you hope has been washed) with a loud toddler or preschool cry while the rest of the world pushes their carts on by. Those are challenging times—where you're forced to parent in front of the audience of your local store.

This has been me.

We were in the store—just for a quick run for cereal and bread and maybe strawberries if they were on sale. Before we went in, I talked to my six- and four-year-old boys and told them what we were getting and that we were getting nothing more. Elijah, the then-four-year-old, was to hold my hand the entire time because he has this tendency to run off (quickly) and check things out.

I knew I was in for a challenge when, as the sliding doors opened, he jumped around and attempted to run and loudly exclaimed, "Look at all the amazing stuff!"

Patience. That's what I kept telling myself.

Patience. Love. But everything was so cool. The berries, the books, the fireworks display at the entrance, the cakes, the ice cream, the hanging balloons, the cereal options. (My kids live in a gluten-free world, limiting their choices to about five cereal options, so you can imagine their excitement when they saw an entire row of cereal). In spite all of that, he was doing pretty good. Until the moment he dashed to look at the cookies (full of gluten) and proceeded to duck in front of me, causing me to trip and him to stumble.

He was irritated that he wasn't going over to those cookies.

I tried to pick him up, and right there in front of the 3-for-$10 frozen pizza display, he decided to sit down and let out a loud "I want to look at the cookies" wail. I'm working on being a *yes* mom, but in this instance, the answer was simply *no*. We can't do gluten in the house, and I'd set the expectations of the shopping trip in the car. I needed to stick with them. I knew people were walking around looking, but honestly, I've learned to not care.

Not in the I'm-just-going-to-let-my-child-cry way, but not care in letting the crying stress me out so it distracts me from parenting.

Your child melting inside the store isn't a reflection of your parenting skills.

But I didn't yell. Instead, I crouched down, looked little Elijah in the eyes, and reminded him of our conversation in the car. About how we were only getting bread, cereal, strawberries, and now one package of pop snaps for the sidewalk for one dollar. He still didn't like it. He was still a wee bit loud.

This wasn't about me looking like I had the perfect child or me talking loudly and screaming at him to stop; this was about me stepping out of my comfort zone and recognizing that he needed me down at that level. There were probably lots of parents wandering in the store. Chances are they've gone through the same thing.

So I scooped him up, right by those pepperoni pizzas, and carried him while Caleb picked up our basket of food. We went to pay, he wanted gum—another cry, but we still left with what we came in for and those $1 pop snaps.

I brought him to the car, buckled him up, and looked in his little face—that face that I love no matter what—and told him I loved him and that I was glad that he got to go with me to the store. I told him about all the times in the store where he did great—in the cereal aisle when I had to say "no" to all those cereals, and by the strawberries, and the fireworks display, and then we talked for a bit about the cookies and why I had to say "no."

He matters more than me looking good.

He deserves more.

Mothers, they will melt down in the store. They simply will. **Shut out the world around you, focus on your child, and do your best. We're not here to judge.** Not at all.

Mothering is hard. And it may not look like this every time one of our kids lose it. This time I was able to keep it together. I may not the next time.

It takes work, a thick skin, patience, and strong arms to carry little ones crying through a store. You will have those days. But you will also have beautiful, creative, and wonderful days.

In fact, right now, as I type these words, my Elijah, my precocious exploring child, is sitting at the table tapping a paintbrush full of black messy paint and splattering it on the table.

"I'm an artist, Momma."

Yep. An artist. In training. Who wanted a cookie full of gluten.

I love him no matter what.

That's what I told myself while I knelt on the floor next to him in the store that morning.

thirty-two

good job

Sometimes at night I will look in the mirror and give myself an "F" for my day of mothering. Well, maybe a "D" and rarely a "C" and even more rarely one of those high grades that I always seemed to get in school but rarely bestow on myself now.

Like today. Today I would give myself a lower grade than normal if I were to talk with you about it. I'd tell you about the bright red sunburned neck that my fifth grader has because I forgot it was track and field day and the spf 50 didn't hit that neck at 8:01 a.m. I'd tell you that I gave Cheetos to my five-year-old at 8:39 a.m. because he would not stop fussing and I had to get to Goodwill before my first grader's class picnic. I'd tell you that instead of getting laundry done I instead squished that pile down even more.

I'd tell you that I ignored the eleventh cry of "Mooommm!" over something to do with a video game.

Trust me—I know that I could have done better.

And those things are really the surface stuff.

Every night I go to bed thinking that tomorrow I will do better. I'll be more intentional. And less impatient. I'll make a super good lunch and get all my work done and the garage cleaned and, and, and...

And then the real day comes.

Well, truth is this: today I was sitting outside at my first grader's school picnic. We were eating and I looked around and, well, we were all normal. There were organic juices and Lunchables and fruit snacks and juice pouches and fruit cups and Goldfish and do you know what else?

Kids laughing and dads laughing and moms laughing.

Not one parent sat there looking at the other person's lunch, cutting them down and handing out grades for the lunches. In fact, as I chatted with the mom next to me, we both chuckled as I bit down on my peanut butter and jelly on gluten-free bread, remarking this tastes yummy, which led to a whole bunch of us laughing about lunches and just being present.

We were all just parenting. Not grading.

And yet, from lunch to parenting to extracurriculars to whatever variable there is in motherhood, we are so dang hard on ourselves.

Enough, honestly.

Let's collectively acknowledge that motherhood isn't made for wimps. We're all going to have days where someone might as well give us the tiara and crown for awesome mom. But then in the same week, we can feel like the worst mom ever as we explode over things like macaroni spilled on the floor and marker on the wall and late homework.

You see, it's all normal.

All within the sphere of motherhood normal.

So this worst critic thing and not seeing the good jobs we all do? Can we all work together to be kind to ourselves? And to remind each other that strength isn't found in perfection?

Maybe if we stop worrying and thinking that everyone else has it all together, then maybe when we put our tired momma heads on the pillow at night, we can all just go to bed thinking, *I totally did a good job today.*

And sometimes, doing your best or a good job means cereal for dinner or tears in the bathroom or the extra-long way home or two lattes or calling a friend for a chat. Sometimes, doing a good job means that you forgive yourself. It means that you throw marshmallows and sometimes it means bedtime is early or having to say *just wait for dinner* and work super hard to put food on the table. Sometimes it means being tired—so tired—and drinking extra coffee but falling asleep in the afternoons anyway.

A good job doesn't look like Hallmark or a Pinterest Board or the Instagram picture with smiling kids and nothing out of order.

A good job is, honestly, doing our best.

Giving ourselves grace.

Sitting at that picnic with your peanut butter and jelly sandwich, fruit cup, and juice pouch and not caring about the externals but rather just being grateful to connect with another mom.

Motherhood can't be based on society's expectations. You do your mom thing and love your kids and just keep trying. And laughing a bit in the middle.

You are doing a good job. So carry on bravely.

just real

There isn't a perfect mom, a perfect house,
a perfect kid, a perfect life.
There's just real.
And real is one mom after another
after another after another
who wakes up in the morning
and sees those kids who call her mom
and pulls herself up and tries.
She stumbles, but stands up.
She worries, but gives.
She loves.
She mothers.

—Rachel Marie Martin
Findingjoy.net

section nine

———

little things matter

thirty-three

---

out of breath

That's me.

I'm the mom with just one more thing on the to-do list. I've got that running tally in my head of items to check off that seem to roll over to the next day and the next until I'm left with a gigantic pile of dirty laundry that's broaching on becoming the highest point in the house.

I race.

From here to there and back up and down the stairs, to the kitchen, out the front door, to the bedrooms, and to that laundry room with the pile of clothes.

So often I live out of breath.

Motherhood is full of living out of breath. You too?

We look at magazines, books, blogs, and Pinterest boards full of serene moments and yet, oftentimes, the only serenity we get is the four-and-a-half minutes where we race to shower while the cry of "Moooommm!" is heard outside the door. Savor those minutes.

For real. It's OK to condition your hair twice while in the shower when you really need a break.

I'll look at my home, and all the things I could or should have been doing all scream at me in the brief moments when I try to pause. I'll mull over slowing down and then the *mom* cry is heard from the family room, and the racing starts up all over again.

It's exhausting. And yet, somehow, sometimes it is beautiful.

It's beautiful when you strip away the layers of fatigue and out-of-breath moments and look at the amazing power of what you're doing. That would be what you and I and mothers have been doing since time began: we give of ourselves for our children. And so often that leaves us in an out-of-breath place for years.

But it won't last.

There will come a day when we are sitting in our tidy homes—with the throw pillows exactly where they are meant to go, a table with no crumbs underneath and no marker stains on the top, walls absent of handprints, bathtubs without piles of toys, cars without stained car seats, bedrooms with no toys to trip on, hallways without Legos underfoot—and we will miss those days.

You and I will look back on these out-of-breath motherhood days, and we will miss them.

Sure, we probably won't miss the exhaustion or the wishing for five more minutes of sleep. Nor those time when a toddler vomits all over your shirt. Or the mass chaos when all the kids need you at once and you're late and you've lost your keys and no one can find their shoes and your phone is ringing.

Well, that's just normal frustrating motherhood stuff.

We'll miss the little things—the little moments—woven into the normal.

Those rooms that used to be messy with the Legos will be so quiet. Little ones won't come racing into the kitchen wanting just one more cookie or snack or asking questions like, "What's for dinner?" There won't be towels left on the bathroom floor or socks under the bed. No spilled milk. Little things.

Those out-of-breath things will probably become the beautiful nostalgic moments we remember. It doesn't make those times any easier. It doesn't add hours of sleep. But it does serve as a reminder that what you're doing, what I'm doing, in our home or at work or in our car or wherever we are is an incredibly beautiful, brave, noble, and amazing thing.

You may not see it. I miss it so often.

I see my mistakes—I was too short, too impatient, too worried, too quick to compare (oh my, is this a trouble one for me)—and forget to give myself grace. When I am out of breath, I start thinking, *If only I had this or could do that, then I might not live out of breath.*

Truth? Until the day when our homes are quiet, we're probably going to live mostly out of breath.

So rest when you can. **Take care of you while mothering.**

And celebrate the astonishing beautiful normal things you do now.

Giving kisses and hugs. Drawing smiley faces. Cutting sandwiches just right. Making soup. Buckling car seats. Tucking in covers. Whispering prayers. Puncturing juice pouches with a straw on the first try. Reading books. Rocking babies. Texting teenagers. Picking up Legos. Driving here and there. Saying, "I love you."

All those things. Those little things in life matter even in the out-of-breath moments.

Breathe.

You are doing just fine.

And if you need a break—take a shower and enjoy your four-and-a-half minutes of semi-silence.

thirty-four

---

time

If you could read only one letter of mine, this one might be it.

Here's why: let's talk about those kids we're blessed to parent. Those kids who stretch our patience, teach us to count to ten multiple times before we lose our cool, cause us to worry and get no sleep, and sometimes bring a smile of joy to our face as well—they'll grow.

Really fast.

I know, you're probably nodding your head and thinking it's just another one of those letters from moms telling you to embrace every moment and to savor every sleepless night and to rock them over and over because they grow up way too fast. Well, you're kind of right. But this letter goes beyond that. It's not about guilt or showing you all the times you didn't savor every second or telling you to do or be more.

There's so much pressure on mothers to be and do and keep it all together while documenting, savoring, and loving everything. Added to the pressure is this idea that every moment is awesome, but we know that most of them are actually rather normal, challenging, plain, and oftentimes just hard. Motherhood isn't about every moment being perfect—rather it's a collection of moments strung together where often the beauty isn't seen until it's done.

The hindsight is often what makes it beautiful.

You may be sitting there, newborn sleeping soundly, with the years of motherhood stretching out before you like a great canvas of opportunity. Or you may be nearing the end, wondering where all those years went to. It happened to me today as well. I pulled winter coats out of my closet and threw them in a heap in the middle of the living room, getting ready to be put away.

It was my three-year-old Samuel's blue puffy Gap coat that brought tears to my eyes.

It might have helped that the Forrest Gump soundtrack was playing in the background, or that it was turning out to be one of those rare, amazing days when your coffee stays hot, the breeze of spring blows in the window, and the kids don't seem to fight as much. Whatever it was, that coat, that blue-striped coat made me cry.

As I took it off the hanger, I paused—where do I throw it?

It won't go in the pile of coats for next year. It won't fit next year—that blue coat that's gotten two years of wear out. The blue coat that Samuel wore home from Children's Hospital this winter when he finally got to come home after dealing with influenza. The blue puffy coat that matches his eyes. He'll be too big next year. Sigh.

My eyes are full of tears again just thinking about that coat. I want him to grow. I want all my kids to grow. And you do too. You and I, we look forward to the next milestone—the first smile, the teeth, the toddling walking, writing their name, the first day of preschool, memorizing math facts, soccer games, driver's ed, and graduation. They're all milestones—goals—events scattered in the fabric of life with all its crazy moments.

I just didn't think they'd roll around so fast.

It feels like I was just throwing a red 2T coat with three little dogs on the front from JC Penney into the pile. And now that girl, that

17-year-old daughter of mine, is almost grown, almost gone from this home and off to start her own. And that is why the tears rolled down my cheeks today. It goes so fast.

We've all read those words, and people repeat them when you're in line at Starbucks waiting for your soy latte while your toddler throws a tantrum. You know it's coming, yet it seems so far away until suddenly its hits you. That first year races by like a blur and they're no longer an infant. Babies grow.

But I know you know that. We all know it deep down. We wonder if this might be the last night we rock them to sleep in our arms, or the last time they hold our hand in the parking lot, or the last day they race through our front door and call it *home*. That's part of the mother's heart—that tucked-in part of us that sees life race by—and yet we just keep moving.

The words I'd want to tell you to benchmark would be to savor the moment, but more than that: give yourself grace. You know why? Because chances are, when you're in the thick of mothering, you're not thinking about the blue puffy coat that you'll throw in a pile and that won't be worn again. Instead you're thinking how you'll make it to 5 p.m. and get dinner on the table. And that's exactly what you should be doing.

Plain and simple. Don't add all these extra pressures about embracing every single second.

But do allow yourself space to step back, to breathe, and to let some tears fall when you put the coats away. And then do what I did—I breathed in that coat, remembered that sweet little one who wore it, and then dashed upstairs to find the preschooler, and ran outside with him to blow bubbles in the yard.

You move forward. Constantly.

Will it go fast? Absolutely yes. But you can go along with it. And every so often you'll be given that gift of perspective—that moment of *remember when*—and then you'll see what a crazy ride motherhood truly is. That's the benchmark for you right now. Pause, just for a second, and see all you've done—what you've accomplished, the memories cherished, and the ones who call you *mother*. Very few ever will get that honor. Remember that—breathe that in today before you return to the dishes, laundry, sweeping, cleaning, and all those things you do.

Dear mom in the beginning, middle, or end of motherhood: it's not the destination; it's the journey. The journey punctuated with crazy, beautiful moments we often don't see until they're done. Don't worry about trying to embrace every second, but simply live.

Embrace the journey.

take time

Take a moment to see the good.
To remember the smiles.
To remember the moments.
To remember the little things.
To be thankful.
To be grateful.
Take time to see the wonderful
in this world.
The more you see the good,
the more you will inspire others
to see it as well.
Ripple.

—Rachel Marie Martin
Findingjoy.net

thirty-five

---

out of balance

Sweet, sweet mom, don't let others' expectations or the pressures of being out of balance slow you down when you need to push hard.

That's the first thing I need you to know. Because sometimes people will tell you to *enjoy the moment,* and you can't even catch your breath or life is just plain hard.

Life is this unpredictable balance. Sometimes it is beautiful and sometimes it is ugly. Sometimes it is easy and sometimes it is hard work. And sometimes you have to get out of balance to get back into balance.

And no one preps you for those years. No one preps you for setbacks. No one preps you for financial struggles or relationship issues. No one preps you for clawing back in life or for the hard work of reclaiming life. No one.

Sometimes, even though you know you should be enjoying the moment, you are just out of balance. It's like teetering on a tightrope trying to make it across, knowing you must keep going but people are yelling, "Look around, savor the moment!" and you know that you cannot stop your momentum.

You have to keep going.

Sometimes when I was in those years of crazy teetering out of balance, I imagined my family cheering on the other side of the hypothetical tightrope. My eyes were fixed there, on them, not on all the noise.

Because it is easy to listen to those who aren't out of balance and convince ourselves we are messing up or missing out on the present. But the now? It's unique, for you in this time. And, sister, it's not always perfect.

Sometimes the now is messy. Sometimes the now is wearying.

Sometimes the now means sacrificing today so tomorrow is better.

Sometimes the now is working away. Sometimes the now is working at home.

Sometimes the now is lonely.

But, sister, when you are determined to change your life or better your life, you are not only blessing yourself, but your family.

There was a time when I was working my way out of a financial situation after becoming a newly single mom, doing almost everything alone, and I cried often.

I felt like I was failing my kids. Then I messaged my mom. She reminded me that I was fighting for my kids and my family. I fought hard to believe her in that moment, but she was right.

I was in the moment, out of balance, but I was there providing for my kids.

My grandpa was a farmer in Minnesota. And during harvest time, he wasn't playing with us. He wasn't watching the sunset. He wasn't in the barn. He was in the fields, laboring away. He was working for his family.

And that is love.

When you find yourself out of balance, you can still choose to move forward and see the beauty of this life. You will be surprised what a mom can accomplish even when her world is off-balance. But remember there is no shame in asking for support or backup. That is the brave thing to do.

If you feel out of sync, out of balance, know that I see you. I know how hard the battle can be, how hard it can be to keep walking, how much focus it takes.

You are creating a better tomorrow.

Maybe your moments don't look Instagram-perfect.

Maybe your moments are breath by breath.

Maybe your moments are raw.

But when you work and give out of tenacious love and fight for your family, that is an extraordinary moment.

thirty-six

the holidays

Let them see you smile.

During this busy, crazy time when the everyday to-do list gets a steroid boost and the race through the everyday doesn't allow you to even catch a breath—bless your family with a smile. Don't wish away the holidays or let the stress of the holidays rob you of joy.

This is why I suggest a smile, because I am talking to myself.

Just the other day, as the kids were begging me to take out the Christmas lights, I remember wishing it was January 2.

Yet, deep down, I really don't.

I don't like the stressed-out, racing, expectation-driven feeling that December often leaves me with. I am guessing some of you don't either. It's hard to step back, to celebrate Christmas and the holidays when you're running too hard and too fast, unable to enjoy the gift of memories found in these weeks.

Try to remember. Try to hold on to the memories.

Try to remember what it was like, when you were a kid and Christmas rolled around. For me, the days seemed to move slowly—like the molasses we'd drizzle into the Moravian Gingerbread cookies—and everything seemed a bit more magical. I remember the lights, reading stories late at night under the Christmas lights, and the never-ending wonder and anticipation of presents that were carefully placed under the tree, but by the time that Christmas arrived they had been examined closely by me and my siblings.

Kids need that bit of excitement, anticipation, joy, and wonder. And yet so often, you and I and the entire culture become busy and stressed out, like a coiled spring ready to snap.

You have a choice. I have a choice.

Embrace the culture of crazy or choose to be intentional during the holidays. The busy won't go away—unless you decline every invite and shop at the weirdest hours possible. **But you can choose not to participate with a stressed-out schedule and attitude.**

Your gift?

Choose joy in the midst.

Choose to celebrate the little things.

Choose to laugh and to create memories with your family.

Choose to slow down and be happy even on those crazy days.

Choose to not allow stress to dictate your mood.

That's what I'm choosing to do, and I challenge you to choose joy as well.

I'm choosing to bake cookies with all their mess, pull out the decorations, string lights outside, play music, draw names, go to parties, and simply celebrate the season. Even if I feel stress.

The bottom line is this, I want my kids to remember me as the mom who smiled during the holidays—even though I'm sure I'll mess up many times. **Deep down, I want them to see me as the mom who embodied joy.**

That's what I want for you.

love

Live in love, not hate.
Live in hope, not anger.
Live in truth, not rumor.
Live in kindness, not rudeness.
Live in generosity, not selfishness.
Live in peace, not frustration.
Live in joy, not doubt.
Live in movement, not fear.
Live in love.

—Rachel Marie Martin
Findingjoy.net

strength

You don't learn how strong
you are until you are
pushed beyond what
you thought you could
handle and emerge on
the other side
with more bravery,
grace, and
determination than
you realized you even had.

—Rachel Marie Martin
Findingjoy.net

section ten

---

for those days with middles and tweens

thirty-seven

———

when parenting isn't cute anymore

My parenting story isn't cute anymore. It's true. I'm in those years of parenting that just are nitty-gritty-not-redeemable by Instagram. Friends, those middle years and teenage years and young adult years just aren't cute.

It's a great deal of no sleep—not due to waking babes but to me sitting up waiting for them to return.

It's a great deal of worrying and wondering and hoping and homework and tests and sitting in a car while your heart is pounding out your chest while you're yelling "Brake, brake, brake!"

It's a great deal of amazing talks and deafening silence. Oh, the silence. No one told me about the silence. Who would have thought that there would be a day when I wished for a bit of noise?

It's a great deal of feeling alone and wondering, just like you did when they are young, if you are making the right choice. The choices, the choices, that part never seems to end.

It's a great deal of waiting and cheering and hoping and trying and worrying and letting go and being brave.

And it is just not cute.

No more cute sleeping toddlers or fun crafts or goofy faces. No more fun costumes or times pushing swings at the park or all of them in the car, strapped in, with silly songs on.

Ha, now the music is their music, and when I see their memes, I'm like, "I just don't get it...."

It's just different.

But just because it's different doesn't mean it doesn't matter.

It matters in that I am still their mom. Their constant, their safe place, their go-to, their person.

You see, in all of motherhood, the simplest things matter the most: the showing up, the loving, the dealing, the listening, the giving, the caring, the sleepless nights and waiting for texts and loving so deeply.

Years ago I wrote about why being a mom is enough. It still is, even if it isn't cute or adorable or any of that. It matters just as much. And in it all you are still enough, more than enough, in this most unseen and often lonely place of motherhood.

You see, the truth still stands: they need you.

They need you in your tired, imperfect, showing up, loving them unconditionally, setting the rules, being their mom way. You are the pulse, the life, the love.

You are enough.

It's a season. A new season, with love that deepens and pride for them that grows. It may not be as adorable, but oh my goodness, the depth and the ups and downs and letting go—it is all there.

This season, this not-so-cute season matters.

And so do you.

a single step

*There are moments in life
where it feels like you
cannot take another step.
Where you can't see where you
are going. But you keep on.
You keep marching forward.
One step, one step, one step.
And your bravery, your courage
in the small steps
will lead you to new things.
Don't ever overlook
the power of a single step.
Those steps will change
your life.*

—Rachel Marie Martin
Findingjoy.net

thirty-eight

the in-between years

I'm kind of in this weird spot of motherhood. Let's just call it the not-so-glamorous but still stressful but now-I'm-trying-to-find-myself place. In other words, I don't have cute toddlers or fun preschoolers. My youngest is nine, my oldest twenty-three, and I have a collection of kids in the middle.

It's the midlife crisis place that I saw on television growing up. Typically, the dad would get a fancy red car and the mom would be in some room crying or she'd cut her hair crazy while the kids were fighting downstairs. My hair, much to my dismay has lost its fullness, and I find myself scouring Target for conditioners that add extra body. And speaking of body, somehow in this middle crazy space my own body has decided to have a resurgence of those teenage hormones. So while I'm purchasing the thickening shampoo, I'm also over in the acne aisle wondering if Neutrogena still works. Oh yeah, and at CrossFit, I get called "ma'am" by the new people. That never happened when I was in my twenties ... just saying.

Not many books and articles talk about existing in this space— this purgatory, stuck-in-the-middle-but-still-feeling-young-while-still-not-getting-much-sleep of parenting. In fact, that's me, in the agony of hours known as homework—where you can't do anything but wait for the next question which happens every 32 seconds and lasts for thirty minutes.

Get this—the other day I pulled my teenage son's bed out and found a whole graveyard of Capri-sun containers. His wastebasket is in his room, two feet away, and there I was wanting to pull out my remaining hair over the littering. That's what I texted him at school, in all caps for emphasis: IN OUR HOUSE WE DO NOT LITTER.

Parenting in these ages can't so quickly be redeemed by a cute photo on Instagram. I mean, come on, do you really want to see the before and after of a teenage boy's room? Or me sitting in the van *again* waiting. Or my shopping bill at Kroger? Sometimes I go through the line and she's like, "You're here again?" and I just say one thing, "Teenagers." She gives me that empathetic nod, and then the mom behind me with the toddler trying to convince her to buy the M&Ms looks at me, and I know she's either hoping for these years or hugging that little one who still likes to hug her.

So yeah, this space, these nonglamorous years of motherhood. I know that a bunch of you are in here with me. I see you at Kroger and Target and in the school line. I see you cheering them on or waiting to talk to teachers. I see you. And I know it can be lonely and frustrating and tiring. And I want to tell you, just like I told you when we had little kids, that you matter. You are enough.

You are enough if you get frustrated or are chill.

You are enough if you feel a bit lost in this space.

Again: at the end of the day, your kids need you. Now granted, they aren't as cute or as endearing about the ways they tell you so. And sometimes you might be met with silence. Which, take a moment and think about, is what we all craved years ago. Now some days I would give anything for words beyond "I'm fine" and "It's OK" and "Uh-huh."

But that's what these years are about and that's why you matter.

You are their constant. You are the one who loves them behind slammed doors. You are the one helping with 3D cell projects. You are the one pressing the hypothetical brake on the passenger side of the car as your teenager drives. You are also the one saying prayers over and over that you make it to Target *while* they drive. You are the one who will show up for them if they are sick *even* if they said nothing to you in the morning. You are the one adding money to the lunch account. You are the one meeting the boyfriend. You are the one with the tracking app on your phone. You matter. You are their mom.

They still need you. Trust me, they do.

So today hold your head high. **You may be in these years of motherhood with those older kids, but sweet mom—holy moly—these years *count*.** Trust me, I know. My daughter is graduating high school next week. That's a new space in motherhood, but on that day, I am going to breathe a sigh of relief. I made it.

You are making a difference. One Capri Sun container, one carpool line, one homework help, one "I'm here for you," one day at a time. And for that, I say thank you.

From me, another mom in the crazy, unpredictable, just as challenging middle-and-letting-go years, to all of you.

thirty-nine

---

growing up

Dear not-so-little youngest boy of mine,

We were BFFs from the beginning; in fact, I was your first. You adored me in your early years. You would easily fall into my arms and hold my hand. There wasn't a moment where you didn't want to be with me, and sometimes when I would try to get a break, I'd look at you and remember how fleeting these years would be.

It feels like yesterday that all the years of your childhood were in front of me. It feels like all those times I said, "in a minute" were infinite and all those in-a-minutes have added up and here we are, years later.

I still can see that little boy in you. In your smile or the times you are scared and you find me. In the times when I meet you for lunch at school and your face lights up because I'm sitting at the visitor table. I can see it when you're excited about something new on Fortnite or when you and your friends are playing in the yard. I can see it when I check on you as you are sleeping. You still have that same sweet face and curl in the same way.

Maybe we don't hold hands anymore. But we share laughs over YouTube videos.

Maybe we don't play cars. But we run at the park together.

Maybe we don't sit side by side coloring. But we do sit and work (much to your dismay) on math problems.

Maybe the story has changed, but you will always be that sweet little boy of mine.

Oh, don't worry, I'll let you grow. That's what we are supposed to do as moms. Don't fear growing, don't fear letting go.

I've been there when you were sick and when you were well. I've been there for the first day of school and will be there for the last. I've been there when you were scared and when you were on stage. I've been there when you shed tears and when you laughed out loud. I've been there for doctor's visit and hours of homework and trips to the ocean. I've been there on the good days and the normal days and the boring days and the hard days.

Oh how I have been there, my sweet boy. You're my youngest, the baby, the one I'm really having to let go of. No one prepared me for how hard it is to let go of the youngest. But here I am, with you, and now time is moving at a speed I'm just not ready for.

But despite that, I'll be there.

So keep growing. Keep trying new things. Keep loving. Keep going. Keep being you. I'm so proud to be your mom.

And trust me, when you give me a hug, I won't let go first.

grateful

Today, choose to be grateful.
Today, choose to see the good.
Today, choose to be love.
Today, choose to see others.
Today, choose to be kind.
Today, choose to see opportunity.
Today, choose to be a friend.
Today, choose to see moments.
Today, choose.
Be grateful.
Today.

—Rachel Marie Martin
Findingjoy.net

forty

---

holding hands

I'm not good at last times.

I'm much better at the firsts, even though I know the firsts will lead to lasts.

Today, in a whisper—*shh, because I don't really want it to be and maybe if I whisper it won't be true*—today was one of those last time moments in motherhood. A letting go, a release, an exhale. I tried to inhale, tried to be present, but in the breath I could feel the childhood falling away. You try to cling to it as much as you can, but it's there—those moments of fewer toys and not wanting shirts with characters on them and conversations that go, "Seriously, Mom?" and, oh, that independence that is so needed but so hard in the same breath to embrace.

Today I look a last-time picture. There was me, blurry on the left in my yoga pants and Skechers and camo sweater, and my precocious, endearing, spitfire of a nine-year-old on the right. And if you could see it, I would make sure to note: he is holding my hand. Not because I asked him to. Not because he wasn't feeling well. Not because I needed him to.

He asked to hold my hand.

Let that just sink in to your momma's heart for a moment. There comes a day when holding hands with moms is a not cool thing or they think they are too old or it just fades away. But today, today in the late afternoon as the Nashville sun skirted along the horizon, he didn't care about what it meant to be getting older. He in that moment was so excited and happy to be with me that he said the sweetest thing: "Hold my hand?"

At first, I didn't think anything of it. And then as we wandered in that Walmart parking lot on a quest to find the rest of his Halloween costume, I had this deep gut realization that this probably was a last time. He didn't know I took the photo, but as the sun was fading, I knew that my holding hands part of motherhood was equally fading, and I needed just to remember.

I have pictures of so many firsts and lasts. Kindergarten and moving and reading and awards and first big bed and so forth. But the holding hands? My whole world has been a world of holding my children's hands, and here I was at the very end without a picture, a memory, something.

I needed the picture. He is my baby, my youngest, and I was afraid this was it.

In fact, deep down, I believe this was the last.

The last holding hands time.

The last time *he asked* to hold my hand. The last time he didn't care that he was old and holding his mom's hand. The last time.

I am teary with that raw ache of release, with the moment of realization. I can't even remember the last time before that he held my hand. It had to have been six months ago. I thought that part of mothering was gone, and then there was, today, this gift.

Oh my word. Tears again.

You'd think I could let them go more easily than this. After all, my oldest is twenty-two and graduated from college. I wish I could tell you it just got easier and easier. But, friends, every single time, it's this moment, this breath of realizing, *I have to let you go.*

But I'm going to cling to these moments. I am.

When you ask to hold my hand when you're nine, I will say yes.

When you ask to talk to me late at night when you're a teen, I will say yes.

When you have a bad dream and come in my room needing me, I will say yes.

When you call me just because, I will say yes.

I will be there. I will be there for the firsts, my children, and I will be there for the lasts.

As we walked in and grabbed a cart, he slowly let go. And then he was back to being nine. It was like a goodbye to childhood. I looked at him, running to the display, and thought to myself, *You have done well.*

Let them go, sweet moms. They need us to be the ones who encourage them to fly. They need us cheering them on. They need us to not cling so tightly.

Today I let go.

she lets go

She loosens her
grip slowly.
As the years pass
and the little
one grows
her hand unclenches
bit by bit
so one day they
can fly.

—Rachel Marie Martin
Findingjoy.net

section eleven

———

for those days with teenagers

forty-one

---

mom of teens, I see you

I used to write articles about finding peace during the toddler years, however I am much further down the road in my mom journey now. But. I do miss the part about *putting them down for a nap and taking a bit to catch your breath* advice. It just doesn't work with a seventeen-year-old. Sure, you can ground them, but that is the opposite of peace.

Sometimes I'll read articles about surviving the teen years written by others whose oldest aren't even teens. Bless them, but until you come face to face with a slammed door or college applications or sitting up late at night or dealing with boyfriends or girlfriends, you just don't get it. Teenage years can be lonely, hard, and challenging for the heart. Before you worry that this is just another article of hypotheticals, please know that my oldest two are in their twenties and I have three other teenagers.

I had to catch my breath just reading what I wrote. Three teenagers. So, understand that I get it. No phony stuff here. In fact, *I see you.* I know you want to do your best. I know how hard you try and that you just need a friend. That's why I'm sharing with you what I've learned.

- **You need a village.** If you don't have one, find one, create one. If you think you can't find one, search Facebook and join a group. Parenting teens isn't for the faint of heart. So often it feels isolating; there are moments where you think, *Am I the only one who doesn't have a clue what to do next?* But the village will tell you, *Nope, sister, join us.* Now, listen, the village must be full of real friends, no phonies, because this is not the time that your life will look perfect. This village needs to be full of truth tellers. It is not the time to compare. Teenagers will suck the *perfect* out of your life at times even if they are great and easy to deal with. They are still independent humans trying to figure things out. In fact, that's why this is titled *I see you*, because so often parenting teens feels like trying to tread water and change the world and make dinner and be completely exhausted and no one even knows.

- **Try desperately to remember being a teen.** This one is so hard for me. My teens often think I'm weird or certainly not the coolest, and sometimes I want to be their friend because I think *they're* cool. And now that I don't have to cut their grapes or explain that we don't touch hot stoves, I see them as mini, awesome adults who do cool things or have opinions on life. But despite me believing I'm just as cool as they are, I'm not. So I try to remember those years when my parents, in my head, were embarrassing or annoying or without a clue. And I remember: this is just a season. Trust me, when they turn twenty, parents might suddenly know a thing or two again. Oh yes, one other thing: remember how confusing this time was for you, too, and that memory can give grace. I will say that when they ask to do something with me, this is the time when I jump at the opportunity to make it happen. And I try to act chill when we're out, even though I'm giddy inside.

- **Don't tell parents with young kids, "Just wait until they're teenagers."** Remember what it was like when you only had young kids—overwhelming. Moms (and dads) need love and support for the season they are actually in. That *just wait* phrase minimizes that moment. (Unless it's, "Just wait until you go on the vacation where you can sleep for three days." That's cool.) In fact, let's just not use *just wait* to any parent, because no matter what season you are in, you don't need someone else telling you that this season is easy compared to the next one.

- **You can't make everything perfect, and they will make mistakes.** I kind of hate this one. But it's true. Our kids are under so much pressure. Can you imagine being asked almost all the time, *What are you going to do in the future? Where are you going to study? What are you going to be?* Let's face it: I'm forty-something (gasp), and on many days I can't figure out what I'm going to do tomorrow and the to-do list for today is even overwhelming. I often will step in and save my teens from those moments, especially when they are still trying to figure out their plans. And they will make mistakes. They won't be perfect. They'll stumble. Our job as parents is to extend the hand to help them stand up again and to guide them and help them understand what went wrong and let them know that *we still love them* and *how can we help?* And show up. Sometimes being silent but being there is the most powerful act of all.

- **I know you try, and you love, and there are times you feel alone.** It's scary parenting a teen. It's scary letting go. It's scary having your heart on the line. It's scary watching them drive. So often I read articles that make it seem easy, but let's face it: at moments it's downright scary. And I know that sometimes it doesn't go perfectly and teens rebel. You are a good mom even in those hard places. You are a good mom even if they think you're not. You are a good mom. Just rest in that, just for a moment.

- **Don't fight the emotions.** Letting go is hard. I still remember the day I boarded a plane in Seattle and flew almost two thousand miles away from my oldest. The emotions I felt on the plane were a mixture of elation and fear and hope and pride. We can't just let go as a mom because the kids are older. In fact, those emotions, those bonds, have grown over the years, so the letting go tugs even more strongly at your heart strings. But life is about letting go, letting them grow, and being there when the phone rings at one a.m. and your daughter, on the other side of the country, forgot about the time zone change and is calling to tell you about her day.

I'm getting ready to have my third child graduate from high school. And I can feel her pulling away from the house more and more. Despite my heart being like, *Not again,* part of me feels a deep peace. Not because everything is perfect, but more because I survived. And surviving isn't necessarily a negative thing. In fact, it's a moment in life where I can be proud of the journey because I didn't quit, I loved, and I showed up.

You will survive. I see how hard you give, love, show up, care, wait up, don't quit, pray, worry, and try again.

It won't be easy. I can't sugarcoat that part. Teenage years are *supposed* to be challenging—for all of us. And "challenging" sometimes means growth and learning. Remember, you are not the only one letting go of everything you've known as normal.

They are too.

I was reminded of that the other day when I talked with my daughter and she was panicky about not knowing what to do with her life. In that moment, my memories of being seventeen rushed back and I simply told her, "It's OK."

It's OK. You can do this.

And that goes for you as well. You can do this. It can be hard, but you are strong. You will be OK.

And you are not alone.

I see you.

forty-two

---

tired mom of teens

There's a ridiculously lonely space in motherhood known as the teenage years. Some people act as if moms of teens have all the answers and are on the home stretch.

But let me tell you: If this is the home stretch, it is a bumpy, middle of the night drive, with everyone sleeping in the back of the van. They're always hungry and we always seem to be running late and I'm never quite sure where I'm going. I am also low on gas, the phone is ringing, and when I ask for help, suddenly they're too busy. Oh yes, and I am tired—the kind of tired from not getting sleep for the last twenty or so years and putting your heart out there hoping that all the time you gave and still give matters.

We feel this tension of clinging tightly to the last moment all while proudly letting go and still hoping they make wise choices. We no longer have this tapestry of time in front of us with our kids. Rather, now there are days when the college applications pile up and the bills morph into car insurance for them and our time is spent sitting in bleachers cheering. Instead of wondering when they will learn and grow up, we wonder what in the world they will do because they're *almost* grown up.

And that's pressure too—that *what is your child going to do after high school* kind of pressure. I discovered that the greatest gift we can give our kids is to teach them to figure out their own hearts and dreams and teach them to be financially sound. Sometimes that means college and sometimes it doesn't, and that doesn't determine worth.

I don't have all the answers of motherhood just because I have teens. I had to walk those years. Try, fail, stumble, cry, rejoice, cheer, try, fail, and try again and again.

My oldest is 22, and sometimes I wonder how we made it through. But, truthfully, I use the same strategy when they were young—the same day by day, night after night, good day, bad day, just day by day strategy. I call it fake it until we make it. Because that is the *truth* of motherhood. Who actually knows how to deal with a rebellious teen until you are the one behind the slammed door crying?

We may be seen as the experienced mom but, friend, we are experiencing a new place in motherhood. Hormones, dating, and social issues combine, and this baby *who once thought we were the queen of the world now wonders if we are the worst thing ever.*

And even if our teens don't rebel or slam doors, we are still now on the brink of letting the person who once fit in the crook in our arm walk out of our door to their new home.

Oh, the heart of a mom. You love them so much you let them go.

But back to this teenage article drought: Perhaps there are fewer articles out there about the teenage years because it's just less instantly redeemable than the toddler years. You know, toddlers can scream and make a giant mess, but at the end of the day (at least most of them), they'll come running back to your arms. We (eventually) chuckle about the permanent marker on the wall or make a social media cute post. But I'm telling you, teens are like Febreze, stinky socks, and open chip bags, all smashed into a package with Taco Bell, gym shoes, first dates, and too much cologne. That's not exactly stellar for Instagram.

With littles, you can go online and read post after post about color coding your schedule and making sure nap time fits and wondering about kindergarten. But when you have older kids, those techniques aren't the answer to the emotions you feel when you waited up for them to get home and worried because they were driving.

You never know the mood you'll receive. In some ways it's like the terrible twos but with a whole bunch more attitude—you cannot carry them into a room and give them a time out. It's kind of like playing the lottery: wondering if you'll be ignored or be met with grunts and one-syllable answers.

Fine. Yes. No. Seriously. Fine. OK. (That's the extent of the vocabulary some days....)

You feel like you're winging it. Your teens both drive you crazy and make you proud, and you don't have a clue what to do. Except buy a whole bunch of food at the grocery store because they do eat us out of house and home.

You deal with them questioning your love as you give them more love.

For moms in these gap years of motherhood: I see you. I hear your heart. I feel the bittersweet letting go.

Just because we have teens doesn't mean we don't need friends or that we have all the answers.

We're just in this new phase that might not be as Facebook-worthy. We might not be sharing "first day of" pictures. But some things are the same: lack of sleep, worry, joy, letting go, giving our hearts.

What matters isn't perfection, isn't a car without scratches; it is that you keep on driving. You keep moving.

forty-three

---

letting go of teens

The silence of teenagers can be brutal. I refer to it as the loud silence—so blaring despite its absence.

Sometimes the silence hurts. It cuts so deep. It doesn't let us know if we're making a difference. It doesn't tell us we're important or that we're needed. The silence can feel like a giant schism in the middle of a home.

When they were little, I was always saying, "Shhhh ... not so loud," and now there are moments where I'm desperate for just a word, a sound, of "Hey, Mom, thanks."

But so much of the time I'm met with silence, making me feel like I'm all alone.

I've felt it cut deep. I've felt myself wondering, *Does anything I've done matter now?* or, *How can you be so quiet when you used to be afraid to cross the street without holding my hand?*

And yet, it's there.

Not all the time. Each of my kids are different. But still, there are those moments, those loud moments of silence, that make my mom heart ache for those days of me being the best thing in the world.

I forget my own teenage years sometimes, the conflict inside, wanting to grow up but being terrified of growing up. I forget how I thought my parents didn't have a clue, and I didn't know how to articulate my emotions and thoughts. And I forget how I didn't want others to know I struggled.

In the remembering, I experience this take-a-deep-breath moment: *It's not me. It's just a season.*

So instead of taking it personally (which is so hard not to do), I am grateful for the mini adults-to-be sitting in the room with me. I'm thankful that they walk into the kitchen and eat the food and wear the clothes I wash. I am thankful that I pick them up and drop them off. I'm thankful that they need me even if I don't hear it.

In the end, it matters.

Because today, my teen broke his silence when he was sick. He needed me. His mom.

They need you, sweet moms, even when they are silent. Don't take the silence as an indicator of love. Instead, we have to band together and accept it as part of the timeline of childhood (and give each other shoulders to cry on). Some kids are loud and some rebel and some are silent. You are so important, right now, in their lives. You matter, you are their constant, you are their rock. Even if you don't hear it.

Teenagers need love. They need you. Remember that.

So sneak in the hugs when you can and be grateful for the words you get. And keep on being there.

be brave

She is brave.
She tries.
She gives.
She hopes.
She loves.
And
she lets go.

—Rachel Marie Martin
Findingjoy.net

forty-four

---

mom who worries

That's what nobody gets....
I try to explain just the worry, the worry never goes away....
When I'm not worried about him, I'm worried about the fact that
I'm not worried about Haddie. It's just like it never stops.
I cannot stop worrying long enough to enjoy anything.
Kristina Braverman,
Parenthood – *Season 1, Episode 6*

I thought that I was alone in this crazy worry of motherhood kind of tears falling from my eyes while the noodles boiled on the stove and the spaghetti sauce, which was set much too high, left splatter marks on the stove top that I had just deep cleaned.

In 47 seconds of watching a show and listening to someone else describe worry, here I was sobbing.

How could a character on a show that I was streaming through Amazon Prime perfectly describe my kind of motherhood crazy worry? You know, what keeps me awake at one a.m. wondering what I've missed or if I'm messing up, or even silly things like if I moved the clothes from the washing machine to the dryer or if I signed that permission sheet and so on. And on and on and on.

That's the cycle of motherhood worry.

Worry is so isolating. We don't talk much about the worry because then, catch-22, we'll probably worry that we shared too much or that we don't have it all together. Yes, that worry about being the only mom who doesn't have it together.

The worry that we're not doing enough for our kids. Or that they'll be behind. Or we're not a good mom or that lunch isn't healthy enough and someone will see. Or that their coat won't zip or that they forgot their gloves. Or that we don't have enough funds to pay for that field trip or that we're making the right decisions for them or that, you know—all the worry that keeps us awake instead of sleeping, obsessed about whether we're supposed to bring snacks to soccer. The measuring stick by which I judge myself is crazy too short and full of expectations.

All my worry eventually percolates to the surface, and then one day a simple thing can bring me to tears.

You too? Are you like me—sprinting through your days in a never-ending marathon while everyone else seems to have it together? And not only do they have it together while you're simply trying to breathe, but they're also doing yoga and are holding the tree pose, while you're looking for missing socks and, in the process, knock over your coffee—the last K-Cup in the entire house. (I might have experience with that scenario.)

But listen, listen, listen. The television scene didn't end there. It didn't end with her expressing all this worry and feeling the pressure of motherhood. It ended when the gal she was speaking with said: **"You need to cut yourself some slack."**

(It's OK. Let the tears really fall now. At this point I was a blubbering mess and my five-year-old asked if I was OK and I said *yes, yes, yes*, and then I turned down the stove because the red splotches from the spaghetti sauce were reaching epic proportions. But it was as if she were talking to me and saying, *Rachel cut yourself some slack*.)

We are so hard on ourselves. And then we think there is something wrong with us and no one understands the worry. And the truth is that there is nothing wrong with who we are as moms. And that mom worry—well, at the core it's because we want to be good moms.

Do you see that part of it? At the heart we want to be *good* moms.

We want to do our best, make a difference, raise kids who get life, and just do well at this crazy motherhood journey—one full of advice and suggestions and ideas and you should do it this way but until you're in the middle of potty training or dealing with belligerent middle schoolers or saying goodbye to your 18-year-old as she boards a plane, you just don't know.

And so we worry that we're supposed to be doing more and be better and should have known but forget that most things we don't learn until we do them and on and on and on and we miss how beautiful what we're doing truly is.

Now listen, we cannot worry that if we cut ourselves a bit of slack we're not being a good mom. For real. Because, truth, life doesn't need to be full of that worry. Even though I know it will be there because it's so hard to get rid of. But what if today, when we experience that worry, instead of feeling alone or that no one understands, we remind ourselves of all we've done as well?

(And just so you know, I'm not telling you to never worry again, because you'll worry again and then you'll worry that you're worrying again and then you'll worry that because you're worrying about *this* that you should worry about *that*. I know. That's me.)

Remember that you're not alone in this tears-falling pressures-of-expectations-and-worry thing.

the mirrors reflection

Sometimes I see it and am much too
harsh, too critical of the girl
looking in.
I remember the mistakes
and agonize over the wrinkles and
get frustrated over the stumbles.
Yet lately,
I've learned to be gentle.
To celebrate each mark,
to see the strength,
to be proud of the bravery.
And instead of the mirror showing
weakness and things to fix it has
become the place of courage
and love and kindness.
It just depends on how
one decides to see and love the girl
staring back.

—Rachel Marie Martin
Findingjoy.net

section twelve

———

love yourself

forty-five

—————

you are worth so much more

"I'm fine."

I've whispered that to myself and to others when they ask how I'm doing. But cloaked inside the two little words is a lifetime of hiding behind a facade.

"I'm fine" leaves us feeling like we are a fake, and we fall second to everything else.

It's hidden in so many things—this idea that our deep desires and hearts don't matter as much as we would like them to. We love speaking about community and camaraderie and how we all want to fight to make a difference in the world. And then in the same breath, often when it comes to our mom hearts, we just whisper the silent *I'm fine*, and inside we feel lost and hurt and alone and wonder why in the world we're simply not worth fighting for.

The truth is this—you *are* worth fighting for.

Don't forget about the desires of your heart and all the things you love in the middle of this crazy journey of life. We carry heavy expectations as moms and women. We believe that we have to appear to keep it together and that part of being a mom is denying us, in a way, for a season.

Think about it. We give up sleep. For some, our body has grown babies, and for others, our heart has birthed babies into our lives. We get wrinkles and tired, puffy eyes, and our bodies hug and work and give. We give up stuff so our kids can have a better life. We work hard doing the same thing over and over. And deep down there's a desire to know that our hearts matter.

No one goes through a childhood thinking that they want to be lost in the shadows. Yet motherhood, life, and love are often a journey of being in the shadows. And sometimes if we are not careful, mother-hood can lead to forgetting about ourselves in a slow fade of *I'm fine* and *It doesn't really matter*. Then in the midst of our comfortable (or not so comfortable) life, our identity slowly disappears.

Let's not be a generation that disappears.

The paints sit. The pens don't write. The running shoes gather dust. The cookbooks go to the garage sale pile. The music papers vanish. The times with friends trickle away. The stuff we once loved we no longer have time for. Our days are filled with things that we think will fill those spaces, and yet the spaces are still there.

So what's the antidote?

It's in fighting for you. And not feeling guilt. No guilt.

What if we decided to remember *us* amid motherhood?

What if we took time for ourself today and spoke truthfully about what we were feeling? We might alarm the next person who asks how we are if we respond with, "I'm exhausted but still kicking" or, "I haven't showered for days but I've saved on the water bill."

Could you take a moment to rest or laugh or have fun again without the guilt? What if you fought for the desires of your heart? What if you dared to dust off the running shoes and run or play the piano or spend time with friends?

What if you remember who you are?

I read all the time about women who don't know what to do when their youngest child graduates. I don't want that for us. I really don't. You are so valuable, and you bring crazy cool to this world—a champion of a woman with this unbelievable heart. Remember you and all the things you love.

Let's nurture that. Without guilt.

Run. Cook. Play. Grow.

And when you find yourself whispering, *I'm fine* to someone else, I want you to step back and really think about those words. Are you just uttering them and not fighting for you? There are times to say "I'm fine," but let me impress on you that the moment you forget *you* in the journey and are content to live in the nebulous day to day of *I'm fine* is the very day you are not fine.

I am proud of you.

I don't know why I felt the need to write that, but I did. Maybe it's because we don't hear those words often. We hear about everything we're supposed to be doing or forgot to do, but rarely do we hear that what we're doing is awesome.

So, from me to you, I am so unbelievably proud of you. I am proud of you for looking at the *I'm fine* moments in your life and choosing to fight for you. I'm proud of you for all the times you give and give for your family. I'm proud of you for the times when you have no energy and you feel like you're failing, but you just keep going. I'm proud of you for loving your friends and fighting for your family. I'm proud of you simply for being you.

You are worth way more than living a life sprinkled of just "I'm fine" everywhere.

forty-six

---

your heart matters

I want you to find it again: a spark of hope of encouragement. But more than that, I want you to know there is someone in your corner. Someone who believes in you. Someone who gets the excuses and understands the chaos and knows how deeply painful it can be to look in the mirror and not know the person staring back.

I know because that once was me.

I lost my heart, but I didn't realize it. I really thought I was being a great mom. I thought I was checking all the boxes on the *live a good life and everyone will be happy, and you are a great mom and successful* checklist. Yet there was this gap, this space, this wondering about myself and my own heart. The things I loved. The spaces that made me laugh.

It would quickly get squashed by cries of "Mom!" and notes from school and spilled milk. So I would tuck that heart part of me, that deeply happy part, down just a bit more, hoping it didn't spill out. And I would throw myself into motherhood. Do more, be more, be better, deny yourself, and all of that.

I starved out my heart, in a way. But in that starving came this bit of me that would look around at everyone else and think, *When will I get to be happy?*

And I hated that space. It was lonely. It felt daunting—having the demands of life and motherhood crowd out my own heart. I felt lost.

You see, sweet mom, I want you to know that it's OK to feel lost a bit in motherhood. It's not because you messed up or you didn't do your job. In fact, you are doing amazing things every day. It's not because you aren't a good mom either. Because sometimes it is easy to think, *If only, I were a great mom, I would be fully happy and satisfied.* But that? That's not true either.

Let's get that straight, alright? Raising humans with their own will and stubbornness is not a simple feat. I guarantee you that every one of us has had to deal with meltdowns in the Target aisle by the candy. And it sucks. Every time. Or the notes from school or the *I hate you—you are the worst mom ever.* Or houses that once were immaculate and look like a bomb went off. Or relationships falling apart. Or money issues. Or insert whatever crazy random chaos you did not sign up for.

But listen: just as you cultivate and fight for your kids, you must fight for your heart too.

Could you imagine telling your kids "Eh, your dreams? Don't worry about them today. You'll get to them someday. They're not important." You wouldn't tell them that because you love them. You must love yourself too.

It is not selfish to fill your heart. To follow your dreams too. You may be mom, but you are also you—unique, beautiful, full of talents and gifts. And maybe right now it's not even about doing crazy things but is rather about just a bit of permission.

Permission to breathe.

Permission to take a night off.

Permission to know that your kids will turn out even if you are not perfect.

Permission to understand that your kids have personalities and make choices that you cannot always control.

Permission to laugh again.

You don't need to ever apologize for being you. For saying no when you need to and yes when it's urgent. The only way you will start to recognize the reflection in the mirror again is when you, yes you, decide that that heart is just as valuable as everyone else's.

Because you are valuable. You are wonderful. You are powerful.

I don't want you to storm out of your life and leave everything behind. I do want you to decide that every single day you are going to do one thing that will make you smile. One thing that could change your life. I'm talking one simple thing.

Can you imagine a year of doing one thing? Suddenly that one thing becomes a story, an adventure, a journey. And in it all you have decided, and you are teaching your children, that your journey, your dreams, your heart matters.

I seriously cannot think of a more beautiful lesson than modeling to our children to value our hearts.

It starts with you, sweet mom.

I wrote this because I believe in you. I truly deeply do. I may not know you, I may never meet you face to face, but my calling, my journey, my heart is to speak a word of truth.

Dare to dream. Be brave. Fight for your heart.

Because this is your story, your life, your journey too.

forty-seven

---

be fearless

To live fearless means to decide that today is a gift, that the past was a lesson but to let it go, and that tomorrow is an amazing opportunity.

To be a fearless mom means to decide to rise, to give, to fight for your heart, and to not allow all the baggage and fears and worry define worth. Because deep down, you are enough, you are worth it, you make a difference—you just need to live knowing that truth. And that? That is why I've made this list of traits of a fearless mom. Because this is you.

You just needed the reminder of these eight things fearless moms do.

1. **They see where they stood up—not where they fell.** It's easy to forget the strength in standing up and trying again and again and again. When we live fearless, we can see the beauty of us in the everyday—where we wake, give, and love. That is you. Every single day. Don't doubt me, because right now, you are reading these words. And that means you pushed through another day. In fact, your track record for making it through the bad days is 100 percent—don't forget that. Ever.

2. They focus on the good. I'm one to talk, as I've spent the last year in a funk. And when you're kind of down it's easy to focus on the hard stuff and become pessimistic. But to be fearless means committing to seeing the positive in one's day—instead of going to the worst or negative, choosing to see and believe in a positive future. So tonight I want you to look at your day and to find *one* good thing that happened. Just one—and it can be that you weren't late for school—and celebrate that good.

3. They know their kids will make mistakes. Motherhood isn't for wimps. And our kids *will* make mistakes. But those mistakes don't define our mothering ability. What matters more is how we react to the mistakes, how we try again and again (see number one), and how we love even in the imperfection. Oh yes, and because they know their kids will make mistakes, fearless moms also know that their friends' kids will make mistakes, and so they love and support their friends in those times as well.

4. They are *real*. I know, I know—the challenge of being in a world that embraces a faux authenticity? But, yes, fearless moms are real. They push their worries and comparison fears over to the sidelines and, instead of apologizing for any mess, welcome their friends in. Only when we do this can we begin to reignite the power of community over perfection. So be honest, truthful, and the type of friend who listens and doesn't judge.

5. They learn. Over and over and over. Motherhood (and life) is truly a lesson in learning. No one was a mom until she became a mom. Yet sometimes I think we live in a world that expects us to have all the answers before we begin. Instead, what if we allow ourselves the grace to not know the answers but rather to stumble around, try our best, and give what we can—knowing that, once again, love and showing up matters.

6. **They do, versus just talk.** It's good to share about the hard stuff, but if we live in a culture of just talking, just complaining, just lamenting, and not doing, then we live stuck. Fearless is without baggage. So pay attention to your actions. Are you doing and pushing for change? Or are you always thinking that tomorrow you will get to what you needed to do today? Life will pass by whether you decide that today is the day you want to change or not. Over the last week a friend of mine was diagnosed with stage IV lung cancer. He is 46. And a dad. And that? That makes me want to live hungry—to *do* versus wait until the stars align in a faux utopian perfection.

7. **They do not forget themselves.** Remember the phrase about oxygen on a plane—how the parent is to put it on before the child? That goes for moms too—in everyday life. We cannot live lives on the back burner, letting the candle burn on both ends. My friends, that just equals burnout. Fearless moms know that taking care of themselves is just as important as getting everything finished on the list. Please, please give yourself permission to take care of *you* every single day and to do something that makes you smile.

8. They know that it takes a village. For most of history, women and moms didn't do it alone. They worked in community with each other. When I visited Haiti, all the children sat in the front of the church, and all of the moms kept an eye on them. There was no judging, no comparing, but rather a group effort to teach the kids the church way. And yet, in our lives here, we go through the motions without asking for or giving help. Let's change that. Let's be a generation of fearless moms ready to help and willing to humbly ask when *we* need help. That will change lives.

This is being a fearless mom.

powerful

*There is
a powerful moment
when you exhale
and let go of
what once was
and inhale
and embrace
the wonder of
what will be.*

—Rachel Marie Martin
Findingjoy.net

forty-eight

_____

love yourself

A couple of weeks ago I stood in front of several hundred women and told them I had an identity crisis and that my hair color fiasco—going from blond to dark —was the physical result of internal turmoil.

I wasn't really expecting to talk about my hair. I was expecting to talk about the power of social media to reach community. But somehow, in the first two minutes, I blurted out statements about the hair. Well, it was perpetuated by the profile pic on the screen with me with my formerly blond hair. So I felt the need to explain. To justify.

"Oh that? That's a lot of bleach. And photoshop. See? No wrinkles on that pic. I kind of feel like I want to walk around with the Nashville Instagram filter on all the time. So here I am now. Like this."

And that's how I started. They all laughed.

And as I stood there sharing about algorithms and appropriate Facebook post lengths, I had this internal battle raging: _What if they liked it better the other way?_

No joke. I worried about that from up front while they were in a room wanting to learn. Isn't that like us as moms and women?

We meet the moms in the school line and we chit chat, and then we go home and wonder what they thought about what we were wearing. We look in the Target carts and either judge or worry that we're being judged. We push our kids to excel and enroll them in this and that and drive crazy hours, and our kids tell us they hate piano or soccer and we tell them to continue on. We look at the school supplies and all the stuff to do and we push and push and push.

But for who? Can we just be real and admit that we're exhausting each other out with expectations?

Sometimes I just want to say, "Eat popcorn for dinner." Or, "Just play on your tablet today. I don't care." And the funny thing about that is, I grew up playing Super Mario Bros all summer long or Tetris, and I appear to have turned out halfway OK. Well, I mean I did have that hair identity crisis thing.

So many of us are working so hard to carry the masks of having it all together all the time that we can't tell what it even means to have it all together anymore. Instead we think that if we just tried harder or did this or didn't eat that or didn't say that, we'd finally reach the "all together" state. We compare our stories—aligning our middles and beginnings and trials and do-overs and finishes with everyone else's stories. And sometimes we apologize for us in the middle of it. We apologize for not being together or having the breakdown or for having kids who made a mistake. We apologize and worry, *What in the world are they thinking of me now?*

And that just keeps us all on guard. A bit afraid of being real. But we all fall. And we get up.

So to all of you, all of you right now in the trenches of motherhood: put down the masks and the expectations and worries and measuring sticks and just breathe.

In fact—don't just breathe. Enough of that.

Love yourself.

Love yourself for messing up. Love yourself for trying. Love yourself for giving. Love yourself for the popcorn for dinner nights. Love yourself for the radical haircut. Love yourself for reading. Love yourself for working. Love yourself for worrying. Love yourself for giving. Love yourself.

Don't waste time comparing and basing that love on what you think others think. In fact, the more we love, the more we encourage everyone around us to be real. To love their stories too.

Not the *having it all together* stories. The real stories.

now

Your time to thrive is now.
Your time to dare is now.
Your time to laugh is now.
Your time to be brave is now
Your time to be you is now.
Your time is now.
Not tomorrow, not next week.
But now.
You have today.
Your now.

—Rachel Marie Martin
Findingjoy.net

section thirteen

———

a celebration of motherhood

forty-nine

---

real picture of a mom

If you and I were together and I asked you to describe yourself as a mother, what would you say?

Several years ago a powerful Dove Real Beauty ad asked women to describe themselves to a forensic artist, who then rendered a picture or sketch based on each woman's description. The images created were much harsher than what the women really looked like. Each was quick to point out the flaws and things she didn't like about herself. Next, another woman described each woman to the same forensic artist, after she had met them in person. The images created then were softer, more empowering, and more beautiful as each woman saw more of the good and not the hypothetical flaws that had made it into the first drawing.

As a result, the images were astonishingly different.

What struck me was how others see us better than we see ourselves. Our kids see us differently as well.

What about motherhood?

What if you and I sat on my worn back deck, and I asked you to describe yourself to me as a mom?

What if I asked you to tell me about your days with your kids?

What would you tell me?

Chances are, if you're like me, that you'd start by telling me all the things you don't like and didn't do right, and where you feel as if you're failing. I'd list many things too: the time I snapped because the cereal was spilled all over the kitchen floor. I'd tell you that I wish I didn't get frustrated because they were trying to be helpful, but I only saw the extra work.

I'd tell you about the times I got irritated over the laundry piles, the sassing back, and the constant work. I'd tell you that my family room floor needs to be vacuumed so please don't go down there unless you enjoy the feeling of smooshed crackers under your feet. (And I'm just telling you, those crackers were never allowed downstairs in the first place.) I'd describe how the little boys' room was a mess again. I'd tell you that I didn't read those books at night. Again.

It's so easy to see the places we feel like we're failing.

You and I and all mothers out there can easily pinpoint our flaws.

But, chances are, if I were sitting there with you and I observed you mothering your children, I would see all the ways you are awesome. I would see how patiently you help your toddler tie her shoes. I'd notice the cute projects posted on your refrigerator. I'd see how you count while you button their jackets. I'd observe when you got down on your knees and looked at your daughter in her eyes and told her how awesome she did that day in school. I'd see all the stuff you probably dismiss as just those normal things of motherhood.

Do you know that in my letter Dear Sweet Mom Who Feels Like She Is Failing, many women emailed and thanked me for putting a picture of my messy sink on the blog? Yes, my sink. That's because that messy sink is real. And it's not a sign of failing. If you and I were sitting on my deck, I'd probably tell you about my messy sink and how I feel as if it is an area where I fall short, because we don't really share the messy sink moments in life.

The messy sink is normal, moms.

If you and I are real with each other, we'll realize that we need to stop seeing the messy sink as a sign of not measuring up but rather as a sign of normal. It's just part of motherhood.

The sink gets cleaned, the dishes get put away, and we do it again. Just like laundry, or spills on the floor and other day-to-day stuff of motherhood.

What if we saw that instead? What if you and I started to look at our own lives with the same filter with which we look at other's lives? What if we celebrated that messy sink? And celebrated that we have a family who provides those messy dishes? What if we celebrated those things instead of being so hard on ourselves?

Does your heart need a bit of grace? hope? Or does it long for that feeling of not measuring up or failing to dissolve and fade away?

That's the true beauty of the real mom beauty sketch.

Today, I want you to start seeing yourself with a lens celebrating everything you do. I want you to start celebrating you and your motherhood journey. I know, it is easier to be negative and lean into comparison, eyeing the craft projects on our neighbor's fridge to see if we're measuring up. Motherhood isn't about measuring up, sweet mother.

It's about wiping sticky fingers, letting them play in the mud, washing clothes, listening to stories about kings and dragons and knights. It's about helping them grow and drying dishes and going to bed exhausted wondering if what you're doing really makes a difference. It's about running behind a kite to help get it in the air and combing knots out of hair and blowing bubbles on the deck. It's about pulling up the bootstraps and hoping you have enough energy to get through the day on the three hours of restless sleep from the night before. It's about hooking up the nebulizer and helping that toddler get good air in her lungs. It's about sneaking a nap in when they're all sleeping and telling yourself that it's the right thing to do—because it is.

Do you see those things? Do you see the beautiful everyday moments in your life?

I want you to see you the real amazing mom that you are.

I want you to see the good you do. The times when you raced around and played. The times when you had enough but still mustered up the sweetest smile.

The times when you gave the last sip of your coffee to the eight-year-old and made his day. The times where you fought for your child and called the parent of the other kid who was making fun of yours. The hours in the car, the nights praying, the minutes in front of the stove cooking, the seconds spent wondering.

All of those add up to this beautiful image of motherhood.

Don't let yours be distorted by seeing all the things you think are flaws. Start to celebrate the beauty. Your beauty looks different from mine and from that of the mother in New Zealand, as well as the mother reading on her iPhone and the mother across my street. We're all different. Beautiful in our own motherhood ways.

Celebrate you. *Your* motherhood journey. *Your* accomplishments.

Those kids who are in your home care about you and love you. They love you. To them, you are beautiful. You are Mom.

My real beauty mom sketch? It's of the real mother.

And that mother is you.

her heart

And she felt her heart
get lighter that day
she stopped comparing.
She stopped letting others
put their too-small-boxes
over her potential.
She stopped listening to the critics
and started listening
to the hope of her dreams.
She started to see her
strength. Her bravery
her beautiful heart.
And in that moment
the impossibilities
felt possible.

—Rachel Marie Martin
Findingjoy.net

fifty

you are stronger than you think

In the trenches. In the valleys. On the peaks. On the road of normal. In seasons of change.

You are strong.

Don't listen to the doubts. Or the voices telling you that you don't measure up, that you don't matter, that nothing will ever change, that what you're doing day after day won't make a difference. Those aren't true statements—they are subtle lies that keep you and me stuck and unable to see the amazing tenacity tucked within.

Let me tell you the truth.

Pulling up the covers and kissing a little one goodnight after the hardest day of your life, matters. Smiling when you have tears in your eyes, matters. Pushing the swing in the hot sun when you have a list of things to complete, matters. Opening the almost-empty peanut butter jar and scraping out the last bit to spread on the bread and give to your toddler, matters. Walking out the door and into an office so that you can buy bread and peanut butter, matters. Pumping gas, driving to soccer, cutting orange slices, baking bread, helping with math facts, taking temperatures, changing the laundry, and going to bed exhausted because you continually give of yourself—that all matters.

That is strength.

Many of you are strong in a world where life is overwhelming and impossible. The money is tight. The marriage hard. The child sick. The normal everyday seems to drive you crazy. You work long hours. You can't find work. You miss work (but let's not talk about that).

To you, dear mother, I say that you are strong.

And for so many of you doing this in a world where life feels comfortable but monotonous and you wonder if what you are doing every single day is making a difference.

To you, dear mother, I say that you are strong and you are making a difference.

For those who don't feel strong and are wondering how in the world to get through the next five minutes much less the end of the day and the baby is crying or the phone is ringing or you are alone and your heart aches.

To you, dear mother, I say that you are strong. Just do one thing to keep moving forward.

The world conveys ideas of it means to be strong and powerful: images of perfect lives, bodies, homes, marriages, children, and front porches. That may sound amazing but it's not real.

Failing and succeeding according to the world's expectations will someday fall in the category of things that didn't really matter. They aren't what people will share about us at the end of our lives.

Amazing lies in getting up again and again and trying.

You are stronger than you think.

So when you stand at the sink with the water tumbling out and the toddler pulling at your leg and you're not sure how to get to tomorrow—much less today—and yet you still get through it all, see? You are stronger than you think. When you look at your day and it seems daunting, overwhelming, even impossible, and yet you get up, get your coffee, and push through, you are igniting the raw amazing strength within you.

Strength isn't found in perfection. It is found in the moments, the minutes, the seconds where you give and believe and try and laugh and cry and mother. It's found in laughter, tears, sighs, hugs, laments, "I love you's," and dreams shattered. It's not in keeping it all together—it's in being real and admitting that life isn't perfect, but that you aren't giving up.

You are fighting.

Strength is an amazing gift you have, even though sometimes you don't see it. Or you've forgotten it. Or dismissed it. Or don't remember.

Believe in you. I do today.

Dear mom, you are strong. So incredibly, unbelievably, amazingly strong.

You inspire me to be a better mom.

fifty-one

trust yourself

For years I traveled for work.

For years I was met with this question: "Isn't it hard on your kids for you to be gone so much?" (My business partner, a male, was never met with that question.)

For years I defended me.

For years I forgot that being a mom means *providing* for our kids. And sometimes it doesn't look like the world of motherhood that has been conjured up in our minds, in media, and in the world.

So I started answering "Yeah, it's hard on them. But they need to eat and I need to provide and I'm doing what I need to do because I love them."

I'm not sure what it is about us moms that others ask us questions about motherhood. From the *how do you do it all?* kind of questions to the looks I get if I'm on my phone while sitting at the park to whatever. I took my kids to the park. I love them. I want them to have fun. And because I work at home I have the freedom to bring my work where we go. I'm not a bad mom—I'm a real mom—providing for those kids who love me.

We live in a world that sometimes seems to judge too quickly. It's a world perpetuated with judgments and unwritten rules—from birth to vaccines to school choice to pacifiers to activities to breastfeeding to whatever you want to think about, there is some kind of rule made about it. And truthfully? There is no right choice.

What about if we cared more about loving each other more than the rules?

What if instead of making presuppositions about working moms that we love them for who they are? What if we loved stay-at-home moms for who they are? Part-time working moms? Moms who only eat organic. Moms who love McDonalds? Fit moms? Moms who homeschool? Send their kids to school? Serve on the PTA? Hate the PTA? Do fancy birthday parties? Don't do parties?

What if we just love us?

As a whole. As a group of women who are given the gift in this world to raise other human beings and try to teach them to do the right thing. Isn't that enough?

So yes, I traveled. Yes, I once stayed home. Yes, I once homeschooled. But none of that matters.

What matters the most is that I love love my kids and try hard and don't forget myself in the journey and try to make a good impact in this life on this planet.

The same is true for you.

You are wonderful for you. Not all the other stuff you might get questioned about.

And if you ever feel yourself defending you, walk away.

the shift

*There is a powerful
shift when you
choose to let go
of what is holding you
back and you
embrace the moments,
the opportunities,
and the people
in front of you now.*

—Rachel Marie Martin
Findingjoy.net

fifty-two

---

this is love

Because of love: a letter to my children.

I have days that go in a circle, when I feel like I get nothing done. I pray for the wisdom of Solomon to solve debates between you. I sometimes feel like I'm going to go crazy. I wish for silence and yet know that silence will come sooner than I think. Because of love.

I wake at six a.m. and pack lunches that so often are half-eaten, thrown away, and most of the times not appreciated. Because of love.

I care about things I used to think were silly. I learn the names of YouTube stars and watch videos about Minecraft and smile and tell you it's cool. I look at the search history on your phone and make rules about media. Because of love.

I listen to your breathing during those times your asthma acts up. I count the breaths and hold you in my arms and debate in my head when is the right time to go in and when I'm just being the paranoid mom. Because of love.

I fight and make hard choices. I count pennies at the grocery store. I stay awake until the wee hours of the morning writing and wake before the sun hits the horizon again. Because of love.

I said goodbye to you and watched you fly away. I tied your shoes and felt the slam of the door on my face when you said you hated me. I didn't give up on you. Because of love.

I open bills and doors and buckle seatbelts and shut sliding doors and try to talk to you in the morning on the way to school. I don't count the silence and one-word answers as a loss. Instead I'm grateful for the time. Because of love.

I vacuum and pick up and fold clothes. Again and again and again. Because of love.

I look in the mirror and gather my resolve. I am tired. I am joyful. I crash sometimes and fall apart. I don't give up. I try over and over. Because of love.

I hope and believe in you. I help with homework. I sit on chairs in teacher's rooms and let my eyes fill with tears as I hear about you. I research symptoms and pray for answers. Because of love.

I watch you sleep and breathe in and breathe out and remember when you fit in the crook of my arm and wonder how in the world time is going so fast. And then at the same time sometimes I wish it would go faster on the crazy days. Because of love.

I know I'm not perfect. I gave up on that long ago. Instead I take what I can and try to be better and give myself grace. And I remember that I'm just expected to do my best. Because of love.

I read and study and compare notes and call friends and ask questions and wonder if I'm a good mom. I worry that I'm messing up. I'm proud of your victories. And cheer for you when you fall. Because of love.

Sometimes.

Sometimes I wonder if what I'm doing is enough. I wonder if you all will turn out well and will look back and think that I was a good mom. I've come to peace that I've messed up because, well, this world isn't perfect. But I've learned to understand that messing up and trying and giving matters. Because of love.

And to you, sister, reading these words—sister with the doubts who wonders if what you're doing really is enough or makes a difference—let me remind you of one thing.

Love.

That love you have makes you an amazing mom. Love makes us wonder if we're doing it right and pushes us to try again. Love gets us up even when we're exhausted. Don't discount that, sweet mom. Motherhood may have those days that are hard and trenches and storms, and those are the moments that make the beauty and the normal beautiful.

Because you love.

You love them.

Let that sink in.

Not all the worries, doubts, fears, and measuring-up stuff that clouds our worth.

Instead remember:

You love.

conclusion

During interviews, I'm often asked what kind of advice I'd give myself when I was the new and younger mom. For many years, I had ideas of what I'd tell her–things like not comparing herself to others, to making sure she laughed, to investing in friendship. But, it hasn't been until recently, in the years following my divorce, my remarriage, and the journey through Covid that my response became crystal clear.

I'd tell her two things.

First, I'd want her to have grace for herself in the journey. This is the kind of grace that is so easy to extend to others but often so hard to remember to give back to ourselves. It's the grace to be okay with trying, to be compassionate on the bad days, to not judge the frustrations, and to see that in all of those moments, there is a beautiful person, that's you, that is giving of her time, her heart, and her spirit for the greater good of her family.

Grace is a powerful and beautiful gift, and I wish I had been kinder to myself for many years. And yet, in the exercising of grace presently, I remind myself that for all those years I gave, I loved, and I did my best.

That's what grace is—it's being willing to shift perspective and being willing to see the good in the midst.

Second, I'd tell her not to forget her own heart, her spirit, and her dreams during motherhood. I cannot think of a more beautiful gift for one's kids than to let them see their mom happy and thriving. I'd emphasize the importance of carving out time, in a very busy schedule, for herself. No one can create that time except for you. And then, finally, I would want her to know that there is no guilt in taking this time.

You are a better mom when you operate out of a cup that is not half-empty.

That is what I've learned.

In fact, I've spent the last five years delving deeper and deeper into the concept of finding joy in life despite the circumstances and the realities we deal with daily. You see, the common denominator we all have is the gift of time. Twenty-four hours each day.

You, my friend, are worth some of that time.

The Happy Mom Pledge was written on one of those days where it felt like I'd move from thing to thing to thing, and nothing was being accomplished and no one seemed to notice everything I was doing to keep my family going. I felt invisible and as if nothing really mattered. But then, when I sat to write (because writing is the way to my heart) I realized that I couldn't look for validation from the outside world. Instead, I needed to learn to love myself in my own story. I needed to decide that happiness was not silly, but rather deeply important.

Every single letter in this book is, in some way, a combination of the advice I'd give my younger self and the truth of the Happy Mom pledge.

You see, you can be your worst enemy or your most powerful cheerleader. I hope you choose cheerleader.

You are the cheerleader for your family, for your friends, and I want you to be that for yourself.

You are worth loving yourself, being proud of yourself, and fighting for yourself.

Finally, I hope these letters inspire you to extend grace to yourself in your story. I hope they make you feel a little less alone. I hope they illuminate the breathtakingly beautiful gift of normal. And I truly hope they reinforce that you are not only a good mom but the perfect mom for *your* children.

Keep trying. Keep loving. Keep showing up. Keep investing. Keep caring. Keep on keeping on.

Motherhood is extraordinary.

~Rachel

PS... One final thing, my next book (coming Fall 2024) is devoted to igniting the fire within you and is filled with inspiration, action steps, and motivation to live your most powerful life now.

happy mom pledge

Repeat after me.

(And if you have little kids, it might take a couple of tries simply because you don't get much quiet.)

I will know that I make a difference. *And, yes, it counts when you get up early and pack those lunches and tuck notes in and wait outside the door.*

I will not compare myself to the mom sitting across from me in Starbucks, the pick-up line, or on Facebook. *That mom is probably comparing herself with you, too, so it might be better if you just said hello to each other.*

I will give myself grace when I stumble. *Sorry, you'll stumble. You'll make mistakes. You'll burn the pizza. But you'll get back up again.*

I will find moments to laugh again. *And it can be laughing over anything. I laughed at myself when I was headfirst in the dryer attempting to remove crayon because I thought I would be supermom and get all the laundry done super fast and super fast meant not checking a nine-year-old's pockets for broken crayons. So I just laughed. And sprayed Goo Gone.*

I will again give myself grace because chances are I won't do everything on this list. *If anyone on here completes a to-do list, it will go on the Guinness Book of Mom Records courtesy of Finding Joy.*

Good luck.

I will not be so hard on myself. *That means it is OK if you make cake balls and they turn into cake mush. It's OK that your birthday decorations are from Target. It's super OK (can we all just stand up and cheer) that you said no to the treat bags.*

I will let the tears fall if they need to fall. *Behind bathroom doors, on the phone, in the car, as you're making lunch, to a good friend. Tears are emotion, and sometimes they need to fall.*

I will be proud of my children. *Put their artwork up even if it doesn't match your decor. Text your teenagers to tell them that you love them. Be proud.*

I will let the handprints be on my windows and not apologize for them. *Having kids means having handprints, sticky counters, and permanent marker in places. Like now, in my home, on my five- and seven-year-old sons' door to their room, where they decided to write their name in black, ultrapermanent, never coming off, you might as well buy a new door Sharpie. At least we all never forget which room is theirs.*

I will say thank you to the baristas at Starbucks. *They are your friends. And at Target. And besides that—our kids are watching us. Always say thank you, as you never know the impact you'll make on someone else's life.*

I will not apologize for not having everything together. *Please don't. Then I have to apologize for not having it together, and then we're both stuck thinking that we always have to have it together.*

I will go to bed at night tired but knowing I made a difference. *If you can remember this before you fall asleep, then yes. Otherwise, wake knowing that everything you do is awesome. Well, cleaning toilets may feel not awesome, but let me remind you of your world if you* *did not do this. See? Awesome.*

I will try super hard to not judge others. *You don't know their circumstances. Maybe what is right in your world isn't right in their world. Love. Don't judge.*

I will try even more super hard to not judge myself. *Um totally yes. (Sometimes the baristas at Starbucks remind me of this. See? Love them.) We're our own worst critics. Enough. The Happy Mom pledge is about learning to give ourselves grace.*

I will remember that my kids will make mistakes. *When they screw up at school, which they will, and you get a note, which you will, it is not a reflection of your ability as a mom. Kids are human too. Help them with their mistakes and do not take it personally.*

I will also remember that my kids do not indicate my parenting successes or failures. *See above. Please.*

I will remember again that I will probably not remember to do everything on the list. *Just another reminder. Remember, we're only human. What matters is that you and I try. Get chocolate and start again.*

I will look for one good thing every day. *Yes, yes, yes. Please this. Look for one thing. I know that life can be incredibly tough and tedious and aggravating, but please look for one good thing every day. Even if it was that your latte was extra hot and awesome or that your three-year-old went to bed without fussing. One thing. And three-year-olds going to bed without an argument counts as five good things in case you were wondering.*

I will be thankful. *Gratitude destroys comparison, envy, and that pesky part of ourselves that thinks we don't measure up.*

I will be me and will pursue the things I love. *Just because you are a mom does not mean that every single thing you do has to do with* mothering. Make sure to cultivate your dreams, your desires, and the things you love too. With no guilt.

I will not feel guilty for the nights when it's popcorn for dinner. *Or macaroni and cheese from the box with the powder that you mix with milk and a dash of butter. Or chicken nuggets. Or pancakes.* You got dinner on the table. *Remember that instead.*

I will not let mom guilt bug me at all, in fact. *Going back to that mom guilt thing. It's way way way too easy to feel guilty and think we're not measuring up. Nope. Not anymore. Mom guilt? We're kicking it to the curb.*

I will tell a friend how great a job she's doing. *Starting now. Us moms need to hear from our friends that we appreciate them. Send them this note and have them be part of this Happy Mom Pledge. No more you versus me versus her. That's not happy. Unity.*

I will see the good in me. *After all you're the only one who knows just what to tell your eleven-year-old who's nervous about a test. Or how to cut the kids' sandwiches in the morning. Or where to find the missing shoe or mitten or homework. Or how to deal with slammed doors or I hate you's and not take it personally. You are great.*

I will know that I am enough, and I will try again. *And again and again and again. That's called strength.*

I will be real. *There is no perfect mom in this world of utopian ideals. There is real. And real is beautiful, powerful, amazing, giving, loving, and awesome. So, yes, that's you.*

I will fight for my heart. *And that means letting yourself be happy again.*

I will love me.

That's the Happy Mom Pledge. Will you take it too?

about the author

Rachel Marie Martin is a champion for moms, the underdogs, and humanity. She believes in the power of each of us to make a difference, to live lives filled with joy, to take risks, and that graciousness and kindness are ultimate gifts. She has been writing online since 2005. Her blog, Finding Joy, has reached over 50 million pageviews. And her Facebook Page, Finding Joy Blog, has over a million followers. She co-founded Audience Industries, a global marketing and training company for creatives, influencers, writers, and podcasters.

Rachel is a published author of multiple books and has spoken worldwide. Her articles have been translated into over twenty-five languages and shared on many international platforms. She's a sought-after podcast guest, speaker, and coach who has dedicated her days to providing a spark of hope through her words and voice.

For her first forty years, Rachel lived in Minnesota, but she now calls Nashville, Tennessee, her home. She's married to Dan R. Morris, and between the two of them and their blended family they share eleven children plus one son-in-law. In case you were wondering, holidays are busy and full of laughter, drama, and memories. In her spare time, you can find her working in her yard, playing piano, running, or spending time with those she loves.

To connect with Rachel, find her at facebook.com/findingjoy

acknowledgements

To my parents: Thank you for teaching me the art of persever-
ance. Thanks also for dealing with my perfectionism and procrastina-
tion. But more than anything, thanks for teaching me what love looks
like - in all things - and that showing up for those you love is the
greatest gift.

To my in-laws, or as you say, in-loves: Thank you for welcoming
me into your family, for loving me like a daughter, for loving my
children, and for believing in me. Thanks for your continual invest-
ment in our dreams. You have made Tennessee feel like home.

To my "circle" friends: For over two years, you have been there for
me as we sat sharing our heart stories. Thank you for listening to me,
for supporting me even when I rambled, and for being there in the
good, the hard, and the normal. I'm grateful for you and that now my
circle of friends includes all of you.

To my Minnesota friend for life, Maria: I have watched you
blossom into the most beautiful version of you. Thank you for letting
me walk by you during your journey and for continuing to walk next to
me during mine. I am always your friend, always forever grateful for
our time together.

To Jen: You were the one who texted me, "SUBMIT NOW" for that
very first letter. I remember texting back in fear because it felt so

vulnerable, and you texted back, "GIRL. HIT SUBMIT." In all caps. Thank you for pushing me off the cliff of comfortable into the valley of vulnerability. That valley brought healing, opportunity, and change. I'm so grateful for our friendship.

To Paula: Little did I know when our paths crossed in Chicago how one day I'd be writing a dedication to you, thanking you for all you've done in my life. Thanks for being the initial visionary behind the book version of this book and investing so much heart into it. Look at what we created.

To Karen: my editor and my friend: Thank you for your belief in me, for your patience with me until I was ready to write again, and for seeing me and helping me become a better version of myself. I don't believe in coincidences but rather believe in timing, and I want to tell you that our paths crossing has been a life gift.